PAM GEMS

Plays Four

PAM GEMS

Plays Four

FRANZ INTO APRIL

PASIONARIA

AUNT MARY

UP IN SWEDEN

Q

QUOTA BOOKS LTD
LONDON

First published in 2022 by Quota Books Ltd. 197 Hammersmith
Grove, London W6 0NP
website: www.quotabooks.com – *email*: info@quotabooks.com
Twitter: @Quotabooks

A CIP record for this book is available from the British Library.

ISBN 978-1-7398894-5-6

Typeset in the UK by M Rules
Printed and bound by Biddles
Picture of Pam Gems courtesy of Jonathan Gems
Cover design: TRISTAN

Available from Amazon, Ingram Spark, Quota Books and all politically correct bookstores.

Pam Gems was born in 1925 in Mudeford, near Christchurch, in what was then Hampshire, on the south coast of England. Her father, a Welsh ex-coalminer, died when she was six years old, leaving her mother to bring up Pam and her two brothers on her own.

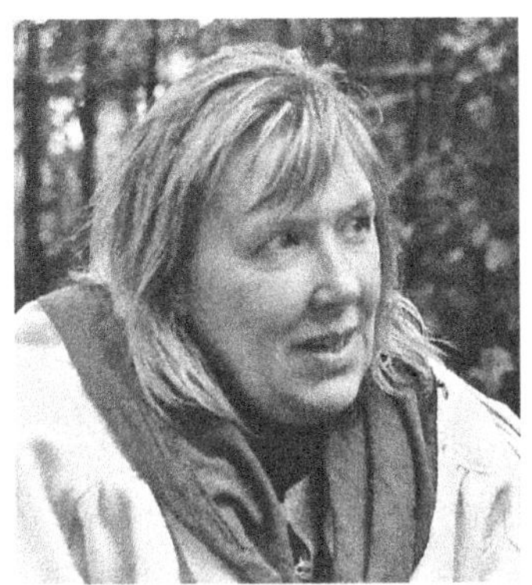

For most of her childhood, Pam's family lived in extreme poverty, reliant on charity from the parish church and the Salvation Army. At eleven, she won a scholarship to grammar school, where she flourished, but left at fifteen to go to work.

World War Two broke out and, in 1943 (when she turned eighteen), she joined the Women's Royal Naval Service, and worked with British and Canadian bomber squadrons. She writes about this in FINCHIE's WAR. After the war, she went to Manchester University, where she studied psychology and met her future husband, Keith.

Always stage-struck, Gems wrote her first play when she was eight, and was an enthusiastic participant in school plays. At university, she joined the dramatic society, wrote skits, produced and directed. After university, she worked in audience research at the BBC – which she loathed – and became part of the 'Ban the Bomb' London beatnik scene, which included Ted Hughes, the poet, Sean Kenny, the designer, and Robert Bolt, the playwright.

After marrying and having her first two children, she and her husband moved to Wandsworth in South London, where she wrote radio plays, beginning a prolific writing career that produced over seventy plays and adaptations. Pam Gems is, without doubt, Britain's greatest woman dramatist, with only Agatha Christie having had more West End productions.

Agatha Christie had ten plays presented in the West End, at a time when the economics of the West End play weren't as prohibitive as they later became. Pam Gems had six, arguably seven, plays produced in the West End. The first was DUSA FISH STAS and VI, at the Mayfair, presented by Michael Codron, followed by PIAF, at the Piccadilly, presented by the RSC, which also produced CAMILLE at the Comedy, and THE BLUE ANGEL at the Globe. LOVING WOMEN was presented at the Arts Theatre, and MARLENE had a successful run at the Lyric. STANLEY, which played to full houses at the National Theatre, was offered a West-End transfer by three managements, but the company turned down these offers in favour of a transfer to the Circle in the Square, off-Broadway, in New York, where it ran for six months.

One thing that especially fascinates in Pam Gems' writing is the prophetic element. She perceived, well in advance, the dangers facing the pampered and decadent West, which now we see unfolding. As Victor Hugo said: 'Adversity makes men and prosperity makes monsters.' Her approach is always positive, however. Like the Beatles' song, all you need is love.

Jonathan Gems

ALSO BY THE SAME AUTHOR

Betty's Wonderful Christmas

Dusa, Fish, Stas and Vi

Queen Christina

Piaf

Go West Young Woman

Camille

Loving Women

King Ludwig of Bavaria

Deborah's Daughter

Marlene

Stanley

The Snow Palace

Mrs. Pat

Ethel

The Socialists

At the Window

The Little Mermaid

After Birthday

Stanley's Women

Next Please

My Warren

The Amiable Courtship of Miz Venus and Wild Bill

The Synonym

The Whippet

The Russian Princess

The Burning Man

A Builder by Trade

The Nourishing Lie

Mr Watts

In Donegal

Cluster

Not Joan The Musical

Down West

The Country House Sale

In The Hothouse

Ladybird, Ladybird

Natalya

Guin for Guinevere

Marine

Who Is Sylvia?

You Should Be Pleased He Likes Me

What Luck

An Ordinary Woman

Cedric and Louise

The Incorruptible

Garibaldi, si!

The Treat

The Leg-Up

We Never Do What They Want

Maytime

Finchie's War

Mabel's Bistro

A Kind of Ecstasy

Guinevere

ADAPTATIONS

The Blue Angel

Sarah B Divine!

My Name is Rosa Luxemburg

Rivers and Forests

Darling Boy

Uncle Vanya

A Doll's House

The Seagull

Ghosts

Yerma

The Lady from the Sea

The Cherry Orchard

The Dance of Death

The Father

Hedda Gabbler

Three Sisters

Behaving Badly

The Odd Women

NOVELS

Mrs Frampton

Bon Voyage, Mrs Frampton

'Society's all wrong. Men should be fighters,
protectors, impregnators. Women are there
to nourish. The further we get away from that,
the more trouble we're in.'

Pam Gems

CONTENTS

LUNCHTIME at the ICA THEATRE

Nash House The Mall SW1

Pam Gems & Frank Hatherley present

WARREN MITCHELL IN

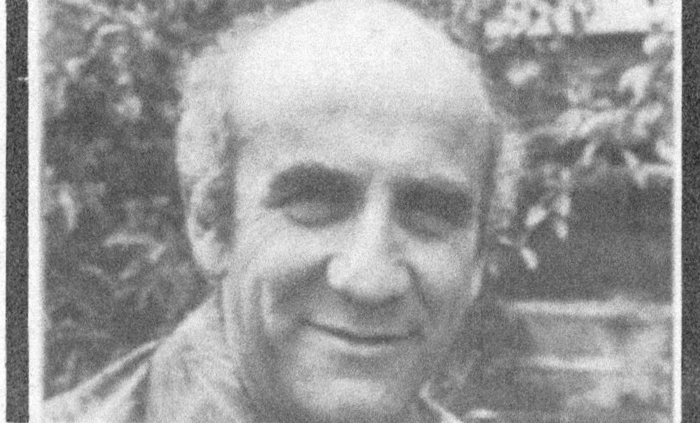

FRANZ into APRIL
by PAM GEMS

with Mark Capri, Alan Cullen, Patricia Franklin & Lise Hilboldt

directed by Frank Hatherley designed by Sally Gardner

1.15 pm Monday – Saturday   Box Office: 930 6393   Tickets 85p (Members 75p)

From 5 December-17 December only

FRANZ INTO APRIL

For Warren Mitchell

Franz Into April was first performed at the Institute of Contemporary Art on 5 December 1977, produced by FRANK HATHERLEY, designed by SALLY GARDNER, and directed by FRANK HATHERLEY.

CAST

Professor Franz Muller	WARREN MITCHELL
April	PATRICIA FRANKLIN
Paula	LISE HILBOLDT
Chris	CHRISTOPHER MUNCKE
Max	SHANE CONNAUGHTON
Wayne	STEVEN DUNBAR

Stage and Company Manager	BARRIE SMITH
Costumes	JEAN MUIR

FOREWORD

After the war, I did a degree course, at Manchester University, in psychology. We studied Freud, Jung and Adler.

We respected Adler, the professional clinician, (he introduced the introvert/extrovert classification) but I was never convinced by Freud – nor did I become a Jung groupie. Years later, I discovered Fritz Perls and, when director Frank Hatherley asked me for a television play, I decided to write about him.

Fritz Perls was a medical doctor from Vienna who specialized in psychiatry. A student of Freud, he left Austria in the Thirties, escaping the Holocaust, and settled in South Africa, and then Australia. From there he went to New York where he practiced until he was forced out by colleagues for refusing to do lobotomies.

Then he went to California and helped to change things.

His basic premise was tough love. He explored with those who came to Esalen (his institute) the challenges involved in growing up. He believed in an existentialist do-it-yourself life, and refused to be a guru. He was a messy eater, groped girls, and was as politically incorrect as you could hope for. Here was a psychiatrist who was not inflated, minatory, exploitative or nuts. He made sense.

On returning from abroad, I was told that the TV production had been cancelled because it was felt that the script was too rude for the general public.

Frank Hatherley, our director, decided to produce it as a stage-play. It opened at the ICA starring Warren Mitchell as Franz. The compassion, humour and insight he brought to the role had people in tears – sometimes with laughter.

We received a rapturous response from the critics and public alike. Warren suggested expanding the text. The expanded version is the one printed here.

Pam Gems

Pam Gems shows considerable dramatic skill in instructing us in the principles of Gestalt Therapy while, at the same time, involving us in a series of flesh-and-blood encounters. We see Franz in action as a doctor trying to get two patients to find their own solutions to their problems; and then we see him as a man irresistibly drawn to a prim English nurse, making love to her, and finally getting her to accept their relationship on a free, non-possessive basis.

Patricia Franklin is very fine as the nurse – the quintessential repressed Englishwoman – while Warren Mitchell had me aching with laughter as the doctor whose philosophy happily licenses his crusading sexual appetite. For its impact and humour, it deserves a much wider audience.

TED WHITEHEAD. *The Spectator*. 24/12/1977

"You must do it for yourself; there are no gurus." That is the philosophy that informs the new Pam Gems play, *Franz into April* (ICA), and a welcome restatement of the truth it is. But the context is startling, for the play is evidently based on, and dedicated, to the memory of Fritz Perls, a very guru among gurus, the man who virtually created Gestalt Psychology, and set off a chain-reaction of liberating therapies. 'Do your own thing' was apparently his coinage.

It is set in a lush, mental-health-farm, where the Director is seen at the start conducting a group-therapy session (in which Lise Hilboldt is quite dazzling as a footloose child-of-nature, not so much scatter-brained as scatter-sexed.) The session is interrupted by a suffocatingly repressed Englishwoman who is not there for help but needs it more than those who are, and the rest of the play consists of a prolonged session of very individual treatment for her, in the course of which the play's title becomes hilariously literal, though the climax takes place behind a discreet row of potted palms.

The writing is amazingly good; muscular, funny, and sharply pointed. The doctor once met Freud, for instance, and hero-worshipped him until he saw the flaw: "Childhood traumas are the lies we tell ourselves in order to justify our refusal to grow up." In a sense, the play is about the fear of, and flight from, maturity (the doctor, with his hedonism and womanizing clearly suffers from it himself, or rather does not suffer, for he recognises and accepts his own psychological weaknesses as Jungianly as he sees those in others – which is presumably why he is able to help them.)

If you like, you can believe that *Franz into April* is a play about a randy psychiatrist ravishing his patients but, in that case, you will have missed the point so completely that you will have proved it.

The doctor is played by Warren Mitchell with a tremendous, guiltless vigour that constitutes a fine advertisement for his theories, and a contemplative resignation that is, though less obviously, another. And Patricia Franklin, as the woman he liberates into life-giving pain, is entirely convincing as she alternates between flight and advancement. The part is a powerful study of human reality, and Miss Franklin's performance does it full justice.

BERNARD LEVIN. *Sunday Times*.11/12/1977

FRANZ INTO APRIL

ACT ONE

ACT ONE – SCENE ONE

California. The early Seventies.

A terraced area, open and airy, with slatted wood and large, stylish plants in low pots, in the Japanese style. There are Kentia palms and possibly a wooden bath tub.

On the blue backcloth are tall palm trees, Hockney style. Overall, an impression of a sophisticated 'simple' life.

An inoffensively designed sign reads: 'To the Pool.'

Down right is a lounging seat with cushions in soft colours. Up centre, a low Japanese table with clutter including a water jug, glasses, tissues, and a tin of talc.

Down centre and left is some other seating, an exercise bicycle, a large rubber ball with hand-holds, and large soft replicas of pencils, balls, and a telephone.

Sitting are MAX, CHRIS, WAYNE and PAULA.

APRIL sits apart.

(NB: If the piece is played in the round, the actors may be sitting in the audience.)

FRANZ, middle-height, bearded, Jewish, not young, bounds on. He is wearing a kaftan in black and brown.

FRANZ

Right ... so ... we begin. Who is for the hot seat? Who wishes to start? Paula? Max? Come on, somebody! Is not so frightening, eh? Is it so frightening? Yes, of course it is. It's not nothing we are doing here. If it didn't take courage, it would be nothing, no? Chris, how about it? We got you this far from the tennis court. One small step, huh? Why not? Give the muscles a rest.

CHRIS

Why pick on me?

But he slouches over to a chair in the centre.

FRANZ

The voice of the true paranoid.

CHRIS

Happy to oblige.

FRANZ

Oh, you're doing me a favour. He's doing me a favour. *(Sudden shout, a habit)* Helping me out! He thinks I need help. No, you are right. I horse around. Maybe I'm nervous too, who knows? *(Slight pause)* So, what's the first thing we notice about Chris?

PAULA

You mean because he said ...

FRANZ

Oh, never mind what he said. That I never listen to – except the tone of voice. Oh, to be a vet! Just to feel the nose. Thermometer in the ass. *(He closes on CHRIS, who stiffens.)* Aha, you see?

WAYNE

He's screwing himself up ...

FRANZ

I enter the force-field. No, don't move. Stay as you are.
Let's try to see what's happening here. My God, Close
Encounters! *(He examines CHRIS like a visiting
Martian.)* What's this? *(Pulling CHRIS'S hand off the
chair.)* A claw? *(He claws his own hand.)* Such power,
tension ... takes energy to do this. I hope you got
plenty. *(He drops CHRIS's hand. CHRIS looks up at
him levelly.)* Ah, he gives me a cold look. Don't come
any closer – keep your distance. OK. So ... tell us
what is happening, Chris. What you feel.

CHRIS

You mean, right now?

FRANZ

No, next year. Come on!

CHRIS

(Taking his time.) I don't know. Nothing.

FRANZ

You don't feel anything? Nothing at all? No itch, pain
in the ass?

PAULA

Come on, Chris.

CHRIS

(Flicks her an irritable glance.) Well, obviously, I'm
under pressure.

FRANZ

You feel pressure.

CHRIS

Sure.

FRANZ

What sort of pressure? You think I'm pressuring you?

CHRIS

Yeah.

FRANZ

Hurrying you up.

CHRIS

You gotta get the show on the road.

FRANZ

Like I said, he's doing me a favour.

WAYNE

(*To CHRIS*) If you don't wanna work – if he doesn't
want to work – you're wasting time!

FRANZ

Yah, yah, but still, he came to the chair. You were
the first. That's always harder. (*To WAYNE:*) Why
didn't you come? Max, what about it, you got glue on
your ass? (*To CHRIS:*) You are the first. A brave man.
So. What you got to share with us? (*CHRIS shrugs,
doesn't reply.*) Come on . . .

CHRIS

I don't know. Frankly I don't know what I'm doing.

FRANZ

'Frankly?' Oh well, if you're going to be frank – who's
Frank? If he's going to be Frank, maybe we do get the
show on the road. Come on kid, some dark secrets,
eh?

CHRIS

Well ... well, frankly ... 'frankly' I just wanted to see
if I could stand up to you.

FRANZ

You wanna fight with Franz? That what you want – a
fight?

CHRIS

Not necessarily.

FRANZ

(*Under his breath, sarcastic.*) 'Not necessarily.' What
then?

CHRIS

I don't know. I don't know what I'm doing ... I mean,
I'm just sitting here getting ready for anything you
might throw at me ...

FRANZ

Go on ...

CHRIS

... trying to think up the best answer.

FRANZ

What is the question? (*A pause.*)

PAULA

It's natural. You're bound to feel anxious.

FRANZ

Ah, anxious! A big word, that, with the psychiatrists.
You feel anxious. You don't want that the
performance goes wrong. You get these feelings,
inside. So, what is it, this anxiety, that we all suffer
so much? I will tell you. Anxiety ... is stage-fright.

Let me ask you … the cats in the kitchen – are they
anxious? Do they suffer in this way? They sleep right
in the middle of the floor where everyone walks.

CHRIS

Maybe they're stupid?

FRANZ

(*Glares*) Sometimes they are fearful that the big
German Shepherd will eat their kittens, so they
move them, but they are not anxious. They are not
sitting in the sun thinking … my God! Suppose he is
eating my kittens now, this minute, or maybe when I
am eating my lunch he will creep across the yard …
kkkk! They have no stage-fright. They don't make
with the scenario. But we do. We are humans, able
to look backwards and forwards in our lives, to see
so many possibilities. What is going to happen? Will
it be good, be bad for us? Applause, or tomatoes?
And so … we fear to tread. You want to give the best
answer, not to make a fool of yourself? OK. But what
is the question? You don't know the question, what
you will feel … if you will like the question. Maybe
the question will even make make you laugh? But
I don't think so, for if you are only thinking of the
answer, how can you enjoy the question? How can you
be spontaneous with us if you rehearse? (*Walks away,
muttering.*) Maybe you want to be like Franz, show off
all the time.

PAULA

Tell him, Chris.

FRANZ

(*Sharp.*) Don't interfere, he doesn't need helpers. Let
him do it on his own. (*To CHRIS:*) And don't worry
about your genitals. They are not about to fall off.

CHRIS'S hands fly from his crotch. A YOUNG WOMAN in the
audience rises and makes her way along the row of chairs.

FRANZ

Just a moment ... just a moment ... You are bored?
Upset? Not getting your money's worth? No, please ...
I would like to know.

APRIL

I'm sorry. I have to leave.

FRANZ

Oh, veddy, veddy Bridish. I didn't know you were
Bridish.

APRIL

What's that supposed to mean?

FRANZ swoops to cut off her exit.

FRANZ

Nothing, I assure you. You are leaving?

APRIL

I'm sorry if that upsets you.

FRANZ

No, no, you don't upset me.

APRIL

I didn't realise it would be so disruptive. I apologise.

FRANZ

But you are still going?

APRIL

Do I have to give a reason?

FRANZ

Purely in the name of research.

APRIL

I see. *(Slight pause.)* I believe I have begun to menstruate. I don't want to stain my dress. Will that do?

FRANZ

The john is just outside. There is a Tampax machine behind the door.

APRIL

Thank you.

FRANZ

You will return to us?

APRIL

Excuse me please. *(She leaves.)*

FRANZ

Hey ... Lana Turner. *(But she has gone.)*

WAYNE

We're wasting time, Franz.

FRANZ

Was she in the class before?

PAULA

No.

WAYNE

So, you lost one. Can't win 'em all.

CHRIS

Look, can I quit now?

FRANZ

Whatsamatter? You didn't even begin!

CHRIS

Can I quit?

FRANZ

(*Absently.*) Sure, sure.

CHRIS

(*Bounding off the chair like a rocket.*) How'd I do?

FRANZ

You see? He still thinks he has to pass a test. Listen, why don't you examine us?

He punches CHRIS hard on the shoulder.

CHRIS

Ow!

FRANZ

Just a little less time on the tennis court, eh ... heh? So ... so ... (*He collects himself.*) Paula.

CHRIS leaves the chair and is replaced by PAULA.

PAULA

(*After a pause.*) I have a fragment of a dream.

FRANZ

(*Sharp.*) No!

PAULA

What I do?

FRANZ

Not 'I have' … 'I am!' I am a fragment of a dream.
Remember? The nouns into verbs. Paula, please!
Don't make a thing out of a process. Life is a process.
Plenty of time for naming it when it is dead.

PAULA

OK. (*She takes out her gum, parks it under her seat.*)
OK. I'm … ah … I'm sitting here … I can hear a fly
buzzing. I have some tension in my neck …

FRANZ

No! You're doing it again! What do you mean, you
'have?' You mean you own it? Show me this tension.
You bought it from the store or something?

PAULA

Sorry. I'm tense.

FRANZ

Just say what is happening.

PAULA

I'm … I guess I'm tensing myself.

FRANZ

Yah! You see? You see how different this is? Not there
is tension, give me a codeine, I'm being battered, it's
not my fault … but … I am tensing myself. We are
not objects, rocks to be kicked about … we are living,
active processes. We tense ourselves. Like a fat man,
or a drug addict … it's not something that happens to
him, it's something he does to himself. He works hard
to achieve it. OK Paula, we forget the dream for now.
Let's do some dialogue about the marriage. I think
you want to talk about the marriage, yah?

PAULA smiles up at him, nods. She turns in her chair.

PAULA

I do love you, Bobbie. *(Slight pause)* You're a very nice guy. *(Slight pause)* It's just, well, it's just that being married, I feel restricted all the time.

FRANZ

OK, change seats. *(She turns slightly the other way.)*

PAULA

(As her husband) But Paula please … you can't talk about breaking up. You know what that would do to me. We're married. I couldn't stand it. *(Turns again.)* But that's what's just so awful, your being so dependent! If I go to the drugstore by myself I feel guilty …

FRANZ

No, no … not guilt. Do it the way we said.

PAULA

Sorry … resent … resentful …

FRANZ

That's right … Guilt is Resentment! Don't say: 'I am guilty' – say the truth. 'I Resent!'

PAULA

Sure. *(As her husband)* Naturally I worry when you're out alone … I … *(in her own voice)* … and he always speaks, you know, in this reasonable voice. *(Turns, speaks as herself.)* But I resent it when you sit in the house worrying about me. You say you don't like to dance then, when I go out with the girls, I feel disloyal … what is more … my family are not boring to me … we have to see them, they're my folks. I resent the way, when we go there you sit in the window and never speak. I resent that! (*Turns in her seat again, speaks as her husband*) Look ... Paula ... I can't pretend something I don't feel. You wouldn't want me to fake our relationship. I try to be honest with you. You say you want it honest between us ... (*She pauses.*)

FRANZ

Note the pause. It's when and where people stop that is important. (*He waves her on.*)

PAULA

(*Speaking as her husband.*) Look, I love you. I want you. I care about you. I'll change ... I'll talk to your old man, if that's what you want. I'll do anything. (*Turns, speaks as herself.*) But that's no good. That's not going to work ... (*Speaks as her husband.*) I know you need me. You were the one who – now I'm into this, I want to ... Lookit, if I'm really nice to you, if I take care of you and play it your way, you won't be able to leave. You won't have any excuse against me. You know how you hate to be alone. You hate it, Paula. (*Pause. A change of voice.*) I'm stuck.

FRANZ

She's stuck.

PAULA

Oh sure, I know. I'm better off than old, sick people. What have I got to complain about? I'm lucky. Yuch.

FRANZ

Say that again.

PAULA

Huh?

FRANZ

Say that last word again.

PAULA

Lucky.

FRANZ

No, the word after that.

PAULA

Yuch?

FRANZ

Again.

PAULA

Yuch!

FRANZ

Louder . . .

PAULA

Yuch!

FRANZ

Louder!

PAULA takes a deep breath. And then lets it out again.

PAULA

I can't. I don't feel it, Franz. I'm putting it on . . .
over-dramatising.

FRANZ

Uhuh? So, where are you?

PAULA

Stuck. I'm stuck in a swamp – you don't have to tell
me, I know! I mean, you can know all about it, but not
be able to do anything. Except feel sorry for yourself.
I don't want to hurt anybody. And I don't want to be on
my own again – have to start off with somebody else.
I'd have nobody to screw with, nobody to cuddle.
I hate sleeping alone. I can't sleep. Just tell me what
to do and I'll do it. I just want out!

FRANZ

Oh really? You don't want to wallow? Wallow – is that
the word? You know it's very nice … wallow … nice
and warm and messy … no?

PAULA

I can't get out!

FRANZ

So, go further in. Think all the time … say out loud –
I'm stuck! Tell the world! Anybody who doesn't know
it already. My God, I think she wants to be stuck. I
think she likes it!

PAULA

(Screams.) Christ, what do you think I'm doing here?
What do you mean, go further in? I couldn't be in any
deeper. What I need is some assistance. Oh fuck, I'm
doing it again.

WAYNE

Over-dramatising.

FRANZ

Making a fuss. About nothing. About your life.

PAULA

Of course, it's not nothing.

FRANZ

Yah, that's why you want help. You think I can help
you? Who is best placed to help you?

PAULA

Oh sure, I know. Nobody can help. I help myself.

She scratches her leg moodily.

FRANZ

Well, that's somebody. That's not nobody … eh?
(Slight pause) So go ahead. Say it.

Slight pause.

PAULA

I'm on my own.

FRANZ

Say it again.

PAULA

(Dolefully.) I'm on my own.

FRANZ

Aw! *(He gets up, gesticulating towards her.)* All alone!
Look at her, ladies and gentlemen, what a pitiful
sight … so sad … so sad …

WAYNE

Aw!

CHRIS

Why don't you shut your fat lip?

FRANZ

Whatsamatter, you feel sorry for her? She's in the
wrong class – you're in the wrong class. (*To PAULA*)
If this was Doctor Reiner's session we would all now
cuddle you, no? Nice big group-grope – avoiding
certain areas. My God, what you're missing, such
love and tears and consolations … but not here. Not
in my class. Sorry to disappoint. What's the matter
with you, Max? I embarrassed you? (*MAX shakes his
head.*) Try the – what is it … where you all sit about
and make with the knots … ?

WAYNE

Macramé.

FRANZ

Yah. Try the macramé next time.

PAULA

(*After a moment.*) You know Franz, you are a bastard.

FRANZ

Yah, I got hairs in my ass, too. (*Shouts.*) What do you
think, I got solutions or something? You think I am
your Daddy? What is it you want from me? You want
candy? A nice shoulder to cry on? Listen, if you need
a hot hand on your butt that's a different matter …

MAX rises majestically to his feet in protest.

WAYNE

Aw, come on …

PAULA

Franz, will you cut that out? Look, if I'm boring you,
I'll leave the chair …

FRANZ

You're not boring me.

PAULA

Then what are you goofing off for? You're not fooling
me. You don't give a shit. What I ought to do is punch
you in the nose and walk right out of here.

FRANZ

So, why don't you?

PAULA

I paid in advance. (*Laughter.*)

FRANZ

Aha! Now we get it! She doesn't want to lose out on
her investment! Profit and loss … profit and loss,
hanh? I put X amount into this relationship – so
many smiles, so many kisses. I played your music …
we ate the way you wanted … now comes the
reckoning! She sees her life in dollar bills.

PAULA

Of course I don't.

FRANZ

Now comes the blaming game.

PAULA

Not at all. Naturally, when you put a lot of yourself
into … it's very sad … I mean, what norms do you
judge your life by? Am I happy? Is this normal? Am I
expecting too much? Not enough?

FRANZ

But you are thinking always in terms of quantity …
this much, that much. The balancing of the books.
The calculation. I give a smile, I get protection.

PAULA

Doesn't everybody?

There is a long silence.

PAULA

(*Quietly.*) You're the expert.

FRANZ

(*Rises.*) And when the guilt takes off its mask – and
when we see it revealed – as resentment – closely
behind this resentment is always the demand. And
now we have some truth, because in the demand . . .
in the demand, we have the only true form of
communication. Help me. Look after me. Protect me.
From what, Paula? From Life? But you are life!
And all the mind-fucking analysis in the world isn't
going to change that. You say the marriage is no good.
So, let the poor bastard go.

PAULA

But he's the one holding on!

FRANZ

Are you sure?

PAULA

Come on!

FRANZ

Maybe you have to take a few chances . . . make a
few mistakes . . . that's no sin, you know. You go from
school to the marriage bed – maybe, after all, you
could stand up by yourself, on your own two legs
and you would not fall over. Who knows? Maybe
you don't need all those soft toys that you keep on
your bed – all these ducks and bears and so. They

are made of nylon. No hearts. (*He looks down at her mesmerically.*)

PROTEINS
> P/A

(*Background, loud.*) It's twelve-thirty, folks . . .

> WAYNE

We didn't get to me.

> P/A

On the menu today we have Cora's bean and celery stew, moussed eggs, mushroom pie and lots of tutti-frutti salads, courtesy of Amy, Pete and Colette.
If you're decadent, the coffee's good, too.

> FRANZ

(*Quickly.*) OK. Put by for me one of Irma's cream tarts somebody . . . until this afternoon, I see you then.
(*He disappears.*)

MAX rises, stands disorientated, then leaves, stiffly.

MUSIC on the P/A.

WAYNE starts dancing, beautifully and professionally. PAULA watches, swaying, while CHRIS morosely stacks chairs and tidies. PAULA moves suggestively at him but he jerks a cushion at her irritably.

WAYNE twirls. PAULA flops back onto cushions, clapping her hands as the music comes to a stop.

> PAULA

Great, Waynie.

> WAYNE

I didn't work out this morning. (*To CHRIS:*) Listen, why weren't you at rehearsal? We're two guys short.

CHRIS

Fuck off.

WAYNE

No Cartier watch for you in your Christmas stocking.

PAULA

(*Calls after him as he goes.*) Wayne, do you want to see my solo? Obviously not. I don't know what I'm doing here. (*To CHRIS:*) Do you? (*He gives her a bleak look.*) I mean, you have to try everything, I suppose, but what is it with Franz? Does he really hate us? And he's got breakfast food all over his kaftan. It's disgusting! I mean, he's smart, obviously, but he needs to take a bath.

CHRIS

(*Shrugs.*) He was kicked out of New York.

PAULA

What for? Malpractice?

CHRIS

He refused to do lobotomies. He wouldn't do surgery on peoples' heads.

PAULA

Franz?

CHRIS

He was working in this complex and the rest of the guys voted him off. He was affecting their incomes. They said he was nuts.

CHRIS

I have to go practice my shots.

PAULA

Yeah, I was watching you crash the pain barrier out
there. Will you be at the show tonight?

CHRIS

You kidding?

PAULA

Aw come on, it's Franzie's birthday. I've bought him
designer deodorant. (*He turns away to go.*) Listen,
Chris ... you know, this aloofness of yours ... (*He
turns, frowning at her.*) I can take it but it gets a little
heavy, know what I mean? Anyway, what do you do
with yourself? I never see you when you're not on the
tennis court. What do you do?

CHRIS

Stay in my room.

PAULA

Why?

CHRIS

Why not?

PAULA

Well not tonight, buster. I'm helping with catering.
You're in for a treat, believe me. Listen, I'll meet you
by the pool at ten thirty. OK?

She goes.

CHRIS watches her without expression. A plant has fallen over. He
notices, picks it up, pushes the plant into place, and pats down the
earth with care. He straightens up, looking round swiftly to make
sure he has not been observed, hoicks up his jeans and goes.

A pause.

APRIL appears in a plain white towelling robe, carrying a towel and cap. She's on her way to the pool. She pauses and, being alone, takes a quick look at the toys, with a detached curiosity. On a whim, she picks up the software telephone and puts it to her ear.

FRANZ

(From behind the palms.) Avon calling! *(She jumps as he peers through the parted palms like a cheerful chimp.)* You want to phone home? Send a letter, it's cheaper. *(He throws a large foam pencil at her.)*

APRIL

(Ducking.) Professor Muller!

FRANZ

Franz, Franz. There is no formality here ...

APRIL leans back against the exercise bicycle, fiddling with the brake.

FRANZ

Try it! Here we treat mind and body together, after all, they are one ... Allez oop! *(He helps her up)*. We don't have a heart, we are a heart, no? *(To humour him she peddles.)* You see? ... *(Fiddling with the speedo.)* ... we turn this way it goes hard ... this way soft. *(She moves slightly as he touches her.)* You want it hard ... you want it soft ... Come, try ... *(He puts his hand on her bum. She slaps it away with her swimming cap.)*

APRIL

Look, would you keep your hands to yourself?

She gets off the bicycle, gathers her things swiftly.

FRANZ

I'm sorry. I just wanted to show you the bike, it's
not ... *(He lifts the bike by the seat, lets out a yowl.)*
Achhh!!!

APRIL

Are you all right?

FRANZ

Ach ... ah ... it's mein back ...

APRIL

All right, all right. There's no need to make a fuss.
You should learn to lift things correctly.

FRANZ

Please, don't give me a lecture. Ahh! I think I pulled
a muscle.

APRIL

Where? *(She bends over him.)* There?

FRANZ

No, lower down, lower down ... Ahh ...

APRIL

Ye-es ... sacroiliac. You'll be sore tomorrow.

FRANZ

I'm sore now.

She crosses to the table, talcs her hands, and returns.

SOFT MUSIC on the P/A ... cello, bubbling and alive.

APRIL

Frankly, Professor Muller, it serves you right ... I'm
not one of your patients, you know. Lie still please.

She begins to work on his back. He groans.

FRANZ

Ooh, ahh! You are a physio?

APRIL

I specialised after nursing.

He puts out a hand, touching her leg.

FRANZ

So, we are colleagues?

APRIL

Could you put your arms by your sides, please?

FRANZ

You came with the alcoholic, no? The little movie
star?

APRIL

Miss Valentine made three films last year and did a
world publicity tour. She's suffering from exhaustion.

He rears, making signs in the air, with little explosive sounds.

APRIL

What are you doing?

FRANZ

I'm putting in the quote signs. We had the hand-out
from the studio too, you know. Tell me, why are you
nursemaid to this lush?

APRIL

(Shrugs.) Oh, just for a change.

FRANZ

From what?

APRIL

I was Head of Physical Therapy at the Denver
Cardiology Unit.

FRANZ

My God, heart surgery ... that can be heavy work.

APRIL

I know.

FRANZ

You didn't like your job?

APRIL

Could you put your hands under your chin, please?

FRANZ

(Obeying her.) You don't like the heart?

APRIL

Oh, I didn't say that. (She attacks him more
vigorously, working into muscle.)

FRANZ

Ow! Why did you leave?

APRIL

We-ell ... the bypass was going out of fashion; we were
having to fill up with valves. We were even getting
down to poor people on welfare. (She sighs.) You work
yourself silly trying to get them going, but they don't
do that well.

FRANZ

You know how to cure a bad heart? Talk to the
patient. Better than the knife. Get a man to change
his life, he doesn't need a pig valve.

APRIL

Well, I wouldn't know about that.

WAYNE enters drinking a white liquid from a tall glass.

WAYNE

High protein. (*He watches APRIL work.*) Terrible shape.

APRIL

Oh, I don't know. For a man of his age ...

FRANZ

What do you mean, for a man of my age?

WAYNE

Touché, eh? (*He laughs.*)

FRANZ

(*Rearing up.*) Listen, this is my lunch break.

WAYNE

I can see that. (*He watches APRIL as she resumes on FRANZ.*) What sad shoulders. (*She looks up.*)

APRIL

What?

WAYNE

Your shoulders. They're sad.

FRANZ

Now he's the therapist.

WAYNE

I'm going! (*He goes.*)

FRANZ

(*Calls.*) Say hullo to Momma for me!

APRIL

He seems rather camp. Is his mother here?

FRANZ

Never leaves his side. *(He barks with laughter.)*

APRIL works for another moment, blows her cheeks out, and stops.

APRIL

There. I think that's enough.

FRANZ

Aren't you going to do my front? It's very relaxing.
You're very good at your job, you know. *(She gives
him a dry look, but obeys.)* Ahh, that feels good …
much better.

APRIL

I don't think there was much wrong with you in the
first place.

FRANZ

I am an old man.

APRIL

You don't act like one.

FRANZ

I have a bad heart! By right I should be dead long
ago – if that brilliant Ida Rolf didn't beat me into life
again. Such hands! Not that yours aren't wonderful
too. You know, I think I'll get them to bury me on the
mountain. Ilse is telling me all the time cremation,
cremation, but you know, to be frizzled all up like
Ilse's chitterling when she tries to cook … not so
aesthetic. *(He begins to drop his shorts.)*

APRIL

Hang on! ...

FRANZ

What?

APRIL

What's happening?

FRANZ

You're not going to ... ? Aren't you going to ... ?

APRIL

Certainly not!

FRANZ

Oh, come on ... please ... between professional colleagues. You know you look very nice when your face is flushed.

APRIL

If this is supposed to be professional behaviour ...

FRANZ

Oh, for God's sake! We are doctors and nurses! Can't we play them a little bit?

APRIL

You're just a dirty old man.

FRANZ

So, where's the harm? Even a dirty old man needs to be loved. Keeps him alive. Why did you leave my session? I'm sorry, I don't know your name.

APRIL

Dobson.

FRANZ

Dobson, Schmobson – no! I mean your name, your
Christian name. Your name – if that's not too familiar.

APRIL

It's April.

FRANZ

April. The spring. That's nice. Why did you walk out
on me?

APRIL

I told you why.

FRANZ

Yah, yah. Put me off my stroke, I'm telling you. You
disapprove of our work here?

APRIL

No, no. I'm sure this sort of thing does extend
frontiers. I'd be the first to … I mean, I'm sure you're
serious.

FRANZ

But …

APRIL

It's just that it's all rather rarefied that's all. I mean
(*She gestures round the room*) – all this.

FRANZ

You know, April … I may call you April? (*She cannot
help a grin at the humble formality.*) You know, I too
have worked in public hospitals, for most of my life.

APRIL

Oh, I wasn't questioning your credentials.

FRANZ

Weren't you, little orthodox lady? No, no, the work we do here – don't misunderstand. Because we are not working with schizophrenics, treating mania, this doesn't mean ...

APRIL

Oh please, I ...

FRANZ

Because we choose to work here with people before, not after they destroy themselves. Is that so bad?

APRIL

No, of course not.

FRANZ

I bring here my life experience.

APRIL

Oh, please, you don't have to ...

FRANZ

Is it such an indulgence? These people here, they fascinate me! All immigrant – hybrids! The vigorous children of the bold, the restless ... centuries of deprivation and, suddenly, abundance. No wonder some of them fill their faces like there is no tomorrow. And so many choices! Shall I be President, go to the moon, fuck all the movie stars? No more jackboot, confessional, custom, class. But no more the old grandmother by the fire to take out the wasp sting and teach you how to cheat at cards. To be free to make your own life, that's exciting. But people want experience, all the good things – but the risk? The pain? That's not so hot. If you are going to improvise your life, you are going to make mistakes. At least when you are in prison there is someone to take care of you. When you get outside it's: oh, doctor, help me please, I want this new happiness pill. *(She smiles.)* Oh, help me, who am I? I don't know who I am! Please let me lie nice and quiet on this couch. *(Snarls)* Cut out a bit of my brain if you want.

APRIL

Doesn't sound as though you like psychiatry.

FRANZ

It's not too fond of me – haha. We did a little experiment a while back. Some of my graduate students masqueraded as patients. Got themselves admitted.

APRIL

That's going a bit far.

FRANZ

It was research. And, my God! Three of them they wouldn't let out. Diagnosed as criminal lunatics! The scandal – believe me, ranks closed fast.

APRIL

I'm not surprised.

FRANZ

April, come on, what does it say, traditional psychiatry? Lie down please, tell me your symptoms so I can help you fit in better. Fit in to what? Listen, we had a movie star here last year ...

APRIL

Oh, who?

FRANZ

Never mind ... Seven years with the most
distinguished shrink in LA – a man I know well.
Very impressive. He was hypnotising the movie
guy, only that day he didn't go under, but he played
along, you know, to be civil. And this high-class
psychiatrist, you know what he does when he thinks
the guy is under? He says: "When you are leaving
pay my receptionist your bill in full because she is
too embarrassed to remind you – cash please, no
cheques!" (APRIL laughs.)

FRANZ

You know what they ask me? They say to me: "What
shall we put on the syllabus, Franz, for your course?"
I say "Messing About." "Oh come, old man, a bit
chancy, don't you think?" I say: "So is life."
(Chuckles to himself.)

APRIL

I've no doubt it's all very interesting, if you've got the
time and money to ...

FRANZ

Sure, sure. I too have nursed a ward of incontinent
geriatrics with one drunken night sister. People
die from lack of funds and here we take money,
and your Miss Valentine is paying good bread and
if we did not charge her high enough she would
think us cheapskates – and we need new equipment
and many come without money so your patient is
also benefactor. This was always so with medicine,
which you know. You see, April ... here we break
new ground. Together, not as Doctor and Patient. I

do not treat people. Un- orthodox, hanh? (*His voice
is hypnotic. She shivers and he gently puts a wrap
around her shoulders.*)

APRIL

Thank you. (*He offers her a cigarette, she shakes her
head.*)

FRANZ

They are low-tar . . . ? (*She shakes her head again.*) And
you are right! (*He throws the pack away.*) When will
Franz learn? Food and cigarettes! All my life I have
tried to give up both. All my life I have failed . . . and
I'm a genius! Founder of the new School of Psychology,
which puts Freud where he belongs – as the Thomas
Edison of Psychiatry. You know I knew him?

APRIL

Edison?

FRANZ

Freud! I was student – so brilliant that by seventeen
I was in the university already. So, at the Vienna
Conference they allowed me . . . they promised me . . .
well, in any case, I was determined to meet him. I
went to his house.

APRIL

To Freud's house?

FRANZ

Yah. He didn't let me in, but he came to the door . . .
which was wide open, by the way . . . also every door
in the house . . . I could see right through. No, he was
polite, agreed that I should join his table after the
symposium. You can't imagine how I felt.

APRIL

You admired him?

FRANZ

I worshipped him. He was my Master! Oh, there were
the mistakes, of course. We are not held in a timeless
prison of childhood trauma, as Freud would have
it. Imagine the chutzpah. I am barely shaving and
I'm wanting to say, Freud, you are wrong! I looked
forward to the discussion over the table … the cigar
smoke drifting up, and Freud, Freud nodding at me
with those appalled eyes of his. I wanted to convert –
or be converted, though of course I knew I was right.
(Pause.)

APRIL

So you had lunch with him?

FRANZ

Yah, yah. He was late. But, when he arrives, so grave
… impossible not to be impressed. I was there with
my professor, and Jeff Waites … Dr Shultz from the
gymnasium … others I don't remember. Then begins
the farce.

APRIL

Mmm?

FRANZ

He arrives where we are sitting and first we must all
move – the table is no good. So, I move my umbrella,
my briefcase – in those days we were very correct, it
was all part of the act, I'm telling you. They give us a
table in the corner, for privacy … but no, Freud is on
his feet again, and we must move to the worst table
in the room, by the door, in a great draught; the door

is open, at Freud's request. At last we are served and
he says not a word – not a word throughout the meal.
One sentence, one sentence alone he addresses to
me … I should be so favoured.

APRIL

What was that?

FRANZ

'Would you be so good as to pass the salt?' (*They
laugh.*) Of course, at that time I didn't know about
Freud's obsessions and the claustrophobia and so
on. You know why the couch, this ikon of psycho-
analysis? Freud couldn't bear to look at anyone in the
face. He was too phobic! So … as a result … I cease to
worship. I give up my guru. I give up my leader, my
maestro, and I give up all this crap on the couch for
my own kind of crap. Though at least with Freudian
analysis the patient gets only more and more dead …
unlike these new con-men: the instant new-life
merchants, the quick rebirth boys. Just say the chant
please … scream … No, April, nobody can do it for us.

APRIL

You seem to have quite a following.

FRANZ

Oh yah, I make a fool of myself. But if they listen
to me, I kick them in the butt. Of course, for the
masochists this is bliss, so with them I am weak and
trembling (*Shouts:*) To wake them up!! No, no … no
gurus. You do it for yourself. We are catalyst here no
more. The management accepts no responsibility, and
I can see you don't approve of that. Tell me, your Miss
Valentine, these are her own tits?

APRIL

If you mean has she had plastic surgery? The
answer's no.

FRANZ

(*Whistles.*) Fantastic. You don't like sex?

APRIL

It's not a question of liking or disliking.

FRANZ

You are indifferent.

APRIL

No of course not.

FRANZ

You can take it or leave it.

APRIL

I didn't say that.

FRANZ

You're not a virgin?

APRIL

No. (*She straightens up.*) I think I'll take my swim.
No, no, please don't get up. I just want to do a few
lengths for the exercise.

FRANZ

Well take it easy. The pool is empty for cleaning.
(*He cackles at his own joke.*)

APRIL

I shall go for a walk then.

FRANZ

As you wish, pale lady. Enjoy yourself.

APRIL

(*A flash of flirtatiousness now that she is safely on her way.*) Now, now, don't be catty.

She bends to pick up her things, and is arrested by the entrance of MAX with a tray.

FRANZ

Ah, Max. Thank you, dear friend. You don't forget me.

MAX

Coffee. I have brought you a Danish pastry.

FRANZ

Fantastisch. (*He looks up, smiling.*) You look nice today. Something happy?

MAX stands, and then, very slowly he bends and kisses FRANZ on the cheek. FRANZ smiles, pleased, then busies himself with the coffee. MAX watches him intently.

FRANZ

(*Sips.*) Ah! Perfect.

MAX relaxes very slightly.

FRANZ

And you got me one with the cherry on the top. I always ... (*He puts the cherry to one side.*) ... eat the cherry last. There are those who eat the cherry first, but not me. Except sometimes. Sometimes we break the rules. Why not? It's fun. And after that, maybe time to remake the rules. Somebody has to do it. Maybe it's our turn? Then maybe we throw away the whole Goddam book – make up the game as we play it. That's hard, no? That's the big league.

Pause.

MAX

I don't understand.

FRANZ

Why don't you trust me a little bit? I am, after all,
your professor.

MAX

You make fun of me.

FRANZ

So laugh!

MAX

(After a moment.) I do trust you.

FRANZ

No, no. If you did you would listen to me.

MAX

I do listen.

FRANZ

But you don't hear. Maybe you talk too much to
yourself? Maybe that's why you don't hear.

MAX

I hear perfectly. I don't know what you mean.

FRANZ

Then do for me a little favour, yes? Eat at the third
sitting today, not the second. And choose a new seat.
Sit on the other side, you can see the lake, it's
beautiful. And why not some dessert? A little fruit
maybe? No, I ask too much. Do one of these things.
Just one. For me. For my sake.

MAX

(Slight pause.) I shall, of course, do exactly as you
say.

He gives a slight formal bow, and goes. FRANZ slaps his hand hard
on the table, making the cups and APRIL jump.

FRANZ

God, I don't know!

APRIL

What a mournful looking chap.

FRANZ

(Drily.) You want to cheer him up? You know, that
man – every minute of the day, organised! Two and
a half minutes to brush his teeth, forty seconds
the hair. I go to his cabin for a little visit, what is
he doing? Ironing his socks! You know what his job
is? Inorganic chemistry. It's poetic. *(He rocks with
laughter.)* Inorganic chemistry! These people! They
think if they stop, their arms and legs will fall off ...
that the earth will cease to turn, the sun to rise ...
most of all, that immediately they will be arrested,
tried and convicted. For what? My God, what it is to
be a Puritan! You know what I think? I think the man
who dreamed up original sin, he had an impotence
problem. Has to be. Come, drink.

APRIL

Oh, are you sure?

FRANZ

Only if you promise not to rape me. *(She gives him a
look of honest puzzlement.)* I beg your pardon. Come,
you can have half my Danish.

She joins him, finding a glass for herself. She sniffs at it suspiciously, washes it, using water from the jug, and wipes it with a tissue. All of which he notes alertly. They share the cake and she helps him to more coffee, and gets him a napkin. He is a messy eater.

FRANZ

(*Mouth full.*) This is very nice ... very nice. I love so much this short rest between sessions ... everything quiet.

APRIL

Oh, I'm so sorry. I'm intruding. I didn't realise.

FRANZ

Not at all, not at all, sit down. Believe me, if I had wanted you to go away, I would have said so.

APRIL

But you need to rest.

FRANZ

You don't want to stay?

APRIL

Why should you want to talk to me? I'm not a patient.

FRANZ

You don't want to talk with me?

APRIL

But you're a director, you must have a thousand ...

FRANZ

Oh, Herr Direktor ... zu befehl, mein Herr ... we must not be forgetting with the hierarchies. Fraternisation ist verboten! Bad mark!

APRIL

(*Mildly.*) I am supposed to be working.

FRANZ

Come – be idle . . .

APRIL

I ought to see if Miss Valentine wants me.

FRANZ

Don't worry. She and the Italian boy have found each other. She won't thank you, believe me.

APRIL

I am getting paid.

FRANZ

Sit down. Where's the harm? Maybe we trade a few secrets, eh? April, I don't want that you disappear . . . I think you do that very easily.

She picks up her cup, sips politely.

FRANZ

So . . . tell me everything.

APRIL

Don't tell me you don't know it already. I can see you get the lot out of people.

FRANZ

But not you?

APRIL

There's nothing to tell.

FRANZ

Your life is too ordinary . . . too banal . . .

APRIL

I hardly think there's anything in it that might
interest you.

FRANZ

How do you know?

APRIL

I should think most people who come here have fairly
exotic lives, no wonder they need to simmer down.
Some of us aren't so lucky.

FRANZ

Luck, what has luck to do with it? My God, what's
wrong with you? There's nothing wrong with you.
You're not ill-favoured. I can see most of what you
got ...

APRIL

Look, please! I know all the Americans here go in for
this head-on stuff. I find it a bit much, that's all.

FRANZ

A bit too much out in the open?

APRIL

I'm not sure I'm prepared to bare my soul at the drop
of a hat. Not in public, anyway.

FRANZ

You prefer the privacy of the consulting room?

APRIL

If I needed it, yes.

FRANZ

I was in analysis myself, as a young man. My God!
(He laughs.) Well, at first, I couldn't think of anything

to reveal to the old boy. I would come in, lie down ...
(*He demonstrates.*) All I needed was a chinstrap and
a lily between my thumbs. But soon I realise ... when
I start to confess ... that what I really enjoy is to look
at women's genitals. Suddenly, there is the scrape of
his chair, and he is sitting closer, closer. Every week
I must think up better stories – he can't get enough of
it! In the end, he is waiting mit the schnapps to help
loosen me up. You are a Don Juan, he says, and when
he sees me in the street he lifts his hat! Ach, what
we do to please! You know that the patients of Freud
had Freudian dreams, those of Jung had Jungian
dreams – anything rather than pleasing themselves,
eh? (*He turns, regards her.*) Me, I work in the group,
as in life. You don't care to share with others?

                    APRIL

I don't see there's any fault in being reticent. People
have a right to privacy.

                    FRANZ

Anyway, you got nothing worth sharing.

                    APRIL

Oh, believe me, I've no false ideas about my charms.

                    FRANZ

You believe you are unattractive?

                    APRIL

I'm realistic. (*Slight pause.*) I remember once, when I
was a little girl ...

                    FRANZ

Aha!

APRIL

What? What have I said?

FRANZ

Your voice – when you said 'little girl.' You spoke
kindly of yourself. You liked yourself then. Go on.
What were you going to tell me?

APRIL

Nothing.

FRANZ

Tell me.

APRIL

Oh, it was a long time ago. I was playing in the
backyard. One day, my mother was folding washing
in the sun. I asked her if I was pretty.

FRANZ

What did she say?

APRIL

(Slight pause.) She said no. (Slight pause.) So, I asked
her if I was ugly. She said ... no. She was very good-
looking herself. We were all very proud of her. I was
playing with some seedpods at the time – lupins. She
said not to eat them, in case they were poisonous. So,
I said if I wasn't pretty and I wasn't ugly, what was
I? I thought she was going to say beautiful because
that's all there was left.

FRANZ

What did she say?

APRIL

She said I was plain.

FRANZ gives a little hiss. Slight pause.

> APRIL

I didn't know what she meant. I hadn't heard the word in quite that context. You know how you get it wrong when you're a kid.

> FRANZ

Why did she say that? It's not true.

> APRIL

Oh, I was nothing special. She wasn't a bad mother. I didn't mean that. She was very imaginative. She used to have ideas ... "Oh come on, April, enough of that silly nonsense." Then she'd have a good sing. (*She smiles briefly.*) Lovely voice.

> FRANZ

She's dead now. (*APRIL nods.*) Brothers ... sisters?

> APRIL

A brother in New Zealand.

> FRANZ

Lovers?

> APRIL

Well, there have been ... you know. I did nearly get married, once.

> FRANZ

(*Whistles ironically, then ...*) Nothing going now?

> APRIL

I'm not exactly in my first bloom.

> FRANZ

My God, what has that got to do with it? My God, if screwing stopped at thirty-five, where would we all be?

APRIL

(*Slightly crushed.*) I'm thirty-two.

FRANZ

(*For the first time, we see him out of face.*) Prrh! ...
I ... I don't suggest you look older ... I use figure of
speech. You're skinny enough to look very young.
It's a nice body, believe me ... I've made love to a lot
worse.

APRIL rises abruptly, fetches up by the bicycle, where she fiddles
about.

APRIL

Yes, well, you obviously go in for all that. I've nothing
against it. I could have gone in for ... there are plenty
of ... one night stands – that sort of thing.

FRANZ

But you despise that?

APRIL

In some ways. Take Samantha – Miss Valentine ...

FRANZ

Rather a lot, eh?

APRIL

She's very experienced. I mean, with her looks.
Apparently, it started she can't even remember when.
She can't remember men not wanting her. All the
time.

FRANZ

But they don't want you?

APRIL

Oh, come on, look at me! Bones sticking out all over
the place – bee-stings for tits.

FRANZ

(*Slight pause*) Tell me, why do you dislike your body
so much? You apologise for yourself every time
you move. You ask us to despise your limbs, your
ass … Why do you lay this task upon us? Is it to
demonstrate the cruelty of your mother? For God's
sake, forgive her! Don't bother us with these old
resentments.

APRIL

Nothing of the sort, she was trying to protect me! She
didn't want me to get ideas … ideas that I couldn't …
She knew! She knew what it was going to be like. She
knew I'd have to stick it out, like most people. She was
doing her best for me.

FRANZ

And so you, in your turn, you, too, become the nurse.
You wish to spend your life 'helping others.'

APRIL

I think there are worse things to do.

FRANZ

Trained … efficient … making no demands … just
a clean apron, and your little diary with the padlock
that you carry around. And what happens down
there? What you think you got it for?

APRIL

You know, you're cruel.

FRANZ

And that's why you walked out of my session, no?
Because you were indignant. You're not bleeding. You
don't have a period, do you?

APRIL

No.

FRANZ

So, tell me – why, if you thought I was being so cruel,
why didn't you speak out?

APRIL

It wasn't any of my ...

FRANZ

Oh no, none of my business, as the man said guarding
the gas chamber. Anyway, as you say, you are
reticent. So coarse to speak up – so unladylike. So,
you just leave – 'quietly.' Meantime, you wreck the
concentration of my session, and the concentration of
Chris who, for the first time, was beginning to work
with me.

APRIL

Work with you? You were poking fun at his balls!

FRANZ

Not at all, not at all. I was suggesting that he ... that
there was no reason for him to hide them ... that
they were perfectly OK, all accounted for, and not too
small! And I would have gone on to make my spiel
about size being unimportant anyway.

APRIL

Hah!

FRANZ

What do you mean – hah!

APRIL

What I said – hah!

FRANZ

No, what is supposed to mean, this Hah!

APRIL

It is important! Of course, it's important, size. Only
we have to pretend it isn't just so you lot can get it up.
Honestly, it makes me laugh, the way women have
to . . .

FRANZ

But . . . excuse me, excuse me . . . what do you suggest?
If a man is small, what is he to do?

APRIL

Find a small woman, for God's sake! Really, I don't
know how I got into all this. I'm going to my room!

FRANZ

(*He lumbers after her.*) Please . . . please stay, April . . .
April, don't go, don't go. Ah, you are upset . . .

He murmurs, stroking the side of her face, pulling her down to the
seat beside him. At first, she averts her face, trying to rise and step
round him. Then, suddenly, she starts to cry.

He puts his arms around her.

FRANZ

April . . . you are so beautiful. Forgive me . . . but you
are lovely when you cry. Here, lean on my shoulder . . .
how good your hair smells. What is it? What do you
put on your hair . . . ?

APRIL

(*Into his shoulder, muffled.*) Eucalyptus shampoo.

FRANZ

No really? It's wonderful ... like the woods above
here, the pine woods ... (*He cuddles her*) ... you
must take me there ... I get breathless, but they are
lovely ... mimosa and pine trees ... a lot of small
flowers ... very pretty ... mmm, your hair. You are
a lady, you know that? You have class, April! What
is it about you English girls? You excite me so much.
Do you find me attractive, April? No, I am too old ... I
disgust you ... be honest with me ... I am so ugly ...
I've never been an attractive man for women ...

APRIL

(*Sniffing*) Not at all. Of course you are. You're very ...
you've got a lovely voice.

FRANZ

If only I were taller.

APRIL

No, no, you're all right as you are, really.

FRANZ

April ... April, take off your bathing costume,
please ... I got my hand trapped up your leg.

She rolls back, laughing.

FRANZ

No, please ... you're breaking my wrist ... April,
please, don't laugh so much, please ...

APRIL

I can't help it, you're so funny ... (*She laughs.*)

FRANZ

(Laughing too.) Yes, I am. I am funny man ... yes,
it's true. *(He embraces her and she doesn't seek to
escape.)* Your skin is so white ... beautiful. There's too
much sun here, it's not good for the skin. Do you know
the women with the best skins in the world? Irish,
because of the rain ... such skins. Kiss me.

APRIL

Why should I?

FRANZ

Just once, that's all ... just to make me feel good. *(She
leans towards him obediently.)* Wait.

He takes off his glasses, puts them on the table. She bends and
kisses him, slightly challenged into proving it before she draws
back.

FRANZ

Oh, my God ... my God ... April you are brilliant
girl ... you taste so good, you know ... these American
women they taste all the time of chemicals, God
knows what they do to themselves. *(He hugs her.)*
I should have sought you out the day you arrived
instead of making eyes at that damn drunk employer
of yours.

APRIL

Poor girl. She's frigid. Her father and mother raped
her when she was eight.

FRANZ

(Bark of laughter.) The mother too?

APRIL

(*Little giggle, then . . .*) Honestly, you'll have to help
her. She can't sleep, and every time she behaves badly
the studio gives in to her and that makes her feel
worse. She doesn't know what to do. D'you think you
could help her?

FRANZ looks up from planting little kisses on her palm and
forearm.

FRANZ

You are a queen. The queen of England. I shall
arrange a coup d'état. I shall be king of course.

APRIL

Oh, you old fool.

FRANZ

(*With a quick look at his watch.*) Make a date with me
for tonight, for the party.

APRIL

Party?

FRANZ

For my birthday. You will be my date.

APRIL

Oh . . . well, I don't know about that – anyway, I've got
nothing to wear.

FRANZ

People don't wear anything! I mean, you wear what
you want. Listen, we could be together, go somewhere,
you know? You would like that . . . really . . . believe
me . . .

APRIL

Don't ... you're impossible.

FRANZ

Sure, sure. You'll come?

APRIL

(Picking up her things.) I'll think about it.

FRANZ

I so love European women. I've been so homesick for them! Such cadence ... here they are all on one note. If you whisper little something in the ear they think you got a strep throat.

APRIL

I think you've bewitched me. Is it all part of the treatment?

FRANZ

Not at all, not at all. I like you, I'm attracted to cool blondes. It's the attraction of opposites. No, I mean it. Believe me, I've had a lot of women. I know what I'm talking about ...

APRIL

(Cheerful.) Oh, don't keep showing off!

She goes. FRANZ walks about, in a good mood, which is interrupted by MAX'S looming appearance.

FRANZ

Ah ... Max.

MAX

I have it here.

FRANZ

(Puzzled.) Yah?

MAX

(*Proffering a few pages of script*) It is my
monologue ... I spoke to you ... you remember?

FRANZ

Oh ... yah, yah, for tonight. Mrs da Souta was telling
me you are going to do a turn. What a sense of
humour, that woman ... she is a big bully. (*He peruses
the papers.*) She says that you wrote it yourself ... it's
good ... (*He manages a chuckle.*) Good ...

MAX

It's dreadful.

FRANZ

Yah, it's pretty bad.

MAX

Better for all, I think, that I kill myself.

FRANZ

Not at all.

MAX

It becomes a comedy.

Behind his back FRANZ reacts to this, stifles a laugh.

FRANZ

Max ... my boy ... (*He tries to pat MAX on the
shoulder, but MAX is too tall.*) Why must you, all
the time make impossible goals for yourself, in
order that you smash your snoot in the ice? I know
that you have a sense of humour – not so much as
me, the little Jew from the wrong suburb of Berlin
who thinks he's good with women – but somewhere
in you I discern a truly cosmic merriment. Why
don't you let it out? Why hold back? Sigmund, no

doubt, would have described you as anal, but I
myself . . .

MAX

Was is das . . . anal? (*He breaks into further urgent
German.*)

FRANZ replies in German, using his hands expressively.

MAX

Jah, jah, I understand . . . of the rectum. But I am
always most regular. I am most careful mit the diet.

FRANZ

(*Sour.*) So I noticed.

They move off together. MAX stops short.

MAX

I think that you don't like me.

FRANZ stops likewise.

FRANZ

What makes you say that?

MAX

You have no sympathy. It is wrong to treat without
sympathy.

He stalks off with dignity. FRANZ collapses onto a seat and mutters
to himself in German. Then he rises.

FRANZ

(*Going.*) Also, Franz, don't forget . . . the food here is
good.

He shambles off, looking small, old and unprepossessing.

Fade to black.

ACT TWO

<u>ACT TWO- SCENE ONE</u>

CHRIS enters with fairy-lights. He leaps about dangerously, putting them up. During the next section, he comes and goes with large bamboo poles with Chinese lanterns, which he slots in the floor at an angle. He also brings on a large dead tree in a pot.

WAYNE enters in a hurry. He's wearing a director's visor, which he dashes to the ground.

> ### WAYNE
> Wouldn't you know! I work my ass off rehearsing a row of club-footed . . .

PAULA enters carrying large cardboard boxes, which she sets down.

> ### PAULA
> Oh now, Wayne. Listen, I told you . . .

> ### WAYNE
> I should never have agreed to work with those cripples!

> ### PAULA
> Wayne, will you listen?

> ### WAYNE
> And where's Coral? Have you seen Coral? I don't have Coral, and I don't have a replacement!

> ### PAULA
> (*Screams.*) I'll do it. I've said I'll do it! I told you I'd do it if anyone dropped out. I said all you had to do was ask – why didn't you ask?

He stops dead, and prowls round her speculatively.

PAULA

I can do tap. I told you ... look! *(She demonstrates.)*

MAX enters, and stands stiffly near the exit.

MAX

Excuse, please.

WAYNE

You don't know the routines.

PAULA

I can learn.

MAX

Excuse me ...

WAYNE

There isn't time!

PAULA

OK!!

WAYNE

Maybe if I solo and we go straight into the Joplin ...

MAX

There is no session now?

PAULA

Sure. Could you hold this for me? *(She gives him a flower with a dazzling smile which petrifies him.)* Thanks!

WAYNE

(Helping CHRIS.) Who've you picked out for tonight? Listen, jeans-type will get you nowhere. You can borrow my shot-rayon frontier shirt.

CHRIS

Fuck off.

WAYNE

OK!

CHRIS

I mean it.

PAULA

(*To MAX as he hands her large red poppies to tie on tree.*) Thank you. (*To CHRIS:*) Are you coming tonight?

CHRIS

You kidding?

PAULA

But you don't do anything. I mean, just the tennis. Why'd you come here?

CHRIS

It was my parents' idea.

PAULA

But why did you ... ?

WAYNE

You should have told them – Sorry, folks.

PAULA

(*To CHRIS.*) Why are you here?

CHRIS

(*With the exasperated sigh of a parent for a stupid child.*) I put a dead cat in a girl's bed. 'A morbid act.'

WAYNE

Some mating call.

CHRIS

You kidding? She was a creep.

MAX

(Clears his throat.) You think the professor is
forgetting us?

CHRIS

Who cares.

WAYNE

Maybe he's had a coronary.

PAULA

(To CHRIS:) So why'd you do it? Put the cat in her
bed?

He ignores her.

PAULA

Revenge?

WAYNE

I told you why he did it. Pretty crappy come-on.

CHRIS

What you talking about? You mean screwing? You
talking about screwing?

PAULA

Chris …

CHRIS

Screwing's screwing. What's the big deal?

WAYNE

I was wrong.

CHRIS

What's it got to do with screwing?

PAULA

Chris, will you shut up! You're embarrassing Max.

WAYNE

Yeah, maybe we don't all have your extended experience. (*He jumps, ties a garland.*) When'd you start? Screwing.

CHRIS

Twelve, thirteen.

PAULA

Twelve? Thirteen?

CHRIS

Same as everyone else.

PAULA

I was at a girl's school. We kissed pictures of Steve McQueen. (*To CHRIS.*) Who did you do it with?

CHRIS

Girls mostly.

PAULA

You mean girls in class?

CHRIS

Sure. (*He hops around on the rubber ball.*) Teachers. Coaches. People's mothers. (*He gets off the ball, gangly.*) They're the worst.

PAULA

People's mothers? Why?

CHRIS

They're vicious. About their husbands.

CHRIS flops on the floor. PAULA comes and sits by him. WAYNE decorates the tree. MAX sits apart, waiting for the afternoon session to begin.

PAULA

(*To CHRIS.*) Didn't you ever fall for anybody?

CHRIS

You kidding?

PAULA

What's that supposed to mean?

CHRIS

Who needs it?

PAULA

And who dropped you on your head?

CHRIS

What's the matter?

PAULA

Nothing!

CHRIS

You wanna fuck, is that it?

MAX rises to his feet but, characteristically, is unable to make the next move. He takes a step towards the exit.

PAULA

No! Of course not! Anyway, I'm married.

WAYNE

Don't we all know!

CHRIS

Yeah, what you wanna get married for?

                    PAULA

There doesn't have to be a reason, you don't have to
give reasons. I was pregnant.

                    WAYNE

Why didn't you have an abortion?

                    PAULA

I didn't want to fuck up my tubes. I wasn't on the Pill
because of side effects and altering my consciousness,
so, wham, I get pregnant and all the girls in my
feminist group are saying why, what for, what's
the reason, like it was some sort of aberration and
anyway, I miscarried. But by then, I'd already
chickened out. I was married.

                    WAYNE

What's he like?

                    PAULA

He suffers from P/E. Premature ejaculation.

MAX reacts.

                    WAYNE

Tough. Does he see you off first or what?

                    PAULA

No. I go to the bathroom. When we're together I
simulate. I've never – you know. Come. *(Sighs.)* It
really must be something.

MAX reacts.

                    WAYNE

Get Chris to get you off.

                    PAULA

(To CHRIS.) D'you think you could?

ACT TWO

WAYNE

Sure, he could.

PAULA

Chris?

CHRIS

(*Climbing down.*) OK. But don't expect anything
fantastic.

This is too much for MAX. He wheels to leave, but bumps into
FRANZ who seems unaware of the collision. FRANZ stumps about,
muttering to himself.

PAULA

Maestro, what's the matter?

FRANZ

You know, there's one thing I can't stand, that's a
woman who puts a man down. They think they are
the oppressed . . . (*To PAULA*) If you knew! You don't
understand. How can they understand it? They alla
this . . . and this . . . (*He gestures.*) . . . they walk about,
showing off . . .

WAYNE

What happened? You get in a fight?

FRANZ

It can be very wounding, you know. I never was a . . .
a Gary Cooper. There's no need to be personal. Look,
I don't think I can work with you this afternoon. I'm
sorry that you all came here, and so, and so.

WAYNE

What did she say? Who was it?

FRANZ

Coral.

WAYNE

(*Highly incensed.*) That armpit?! What do you want to mess with her for? Why do you have such terrible taste in women!

FRANZ

I'm not a young man. I can't be choosy.

PAULA

Franzy, stop trailing your coat. It's your birthday.
(*She whispers in his ear. He cheers up.*)

FRANZ

OK, everybody. Please. Museum time! Memory Lane! Wayne, you going to start?

WAYNE

You bet!

He sits in the centre.

FRANZ

(*After a pause.*) Tell us about your mother.

WAYNE

Oh, for God's sake.

FRANZ

Tell us. You're obviously very close. You take her around with you everyplace.

PAULA stifles a giggle.

WAYNE

So what? It's a free country.

FRANZ

She's dead.

WAYNE

Not to me she ain't.

FRANZ

She's sitting on your mantelpiece ... she's a bunch of
ashes in a bowl. She's dead.

WAYNE

Not to me! Well, in one sense she's dead. Dead as
mutton.

FRANZ

Note the tone of voice.

WAYNE

What do you mean? She's not dead in my heart. She's
still my dearest friend. I stick to her standards.
Believe me, when I saw those chalets I almost
cancelled. She'd die! So tacky! The only place
available for her ... I can't put her on the low table,
people use her for an ashtray. There's only that
softwood shelf. It's not even painted, just creosote –
not to mention the coffee stains and cigarette burns.

FRANZ

Listen, you don't have to bother.

WAYNE

What!

FRANZ

Don't bother. Oh, maybe for the onyx bowl, that's
a handsome piece. But forget what's inside. Those
ashes ... they're not your mother.

WAYNE

What do you mean? How d'you mean they're not my
mother. Of course they're my mother! I was there
when she died. I did her hair in the casket.

FRANZ

Maybe you got a little bit of her, that's possible. These
crematoria, they got to watch the costs. You don't get
a personalized service. They burn when they get a
load, usually ten, twelve – depends on the size of the
oven.

PAULA

Franz, what are you doing!

FRANZ

She's probably in there with a coupla bums and a
garment salesman, who knows?

WAYNE

(Slight pause.) You're asking for trouble. (Slight
pause. His voice wavers.) That was totally off.

PAULA

Don't pay any attention, Wayne.

FRANZ

It's the truth.

Pause.

FRANZ

You want to quit?

They lock gazes in mutual hostility.

WAYNE

She was perfect.

FRANZ

What about your father?

WAYNE

(*Dismissive.*) I don't know.

FRANZ

She had no man?

WAYNE

You kidding? She was the toast of New York ... Josh
Logan was crazy about her work. We had a great
time!

FRANZ

Is that why you're full of shit?

WAYNE

It has nothing to do with my mother, look, I don't want
to deal with this ...

FRANZ

So, get off the stage.

WAYNE

What?

FRANZ

This is museum time – we bring out the old turds.

WAYNE

I don't have to deal with ...

FRANZ

So, get off the stage. I don't want to work with you.
You're a dishonest man.

WAYNE

Why are you being so hostile?

FRANZ

You're a saboteur. I don't work with saboteurs.

WAYNE

How can you say that? I'm here to work. I want to
work.

FRANZ

Then cut the chickenshit.

WAYNE

Because I happen to love my mother, that's
chickenshit? Listen … listen, compared to her, you …
you don't even exist.

FRANZ

Say that to them. Say it to them!

WAYNE

All right! *(To the others.)* Compared to my mother
You're all nobodies!

FRANZ

That's not the same thing.

WAYNE

So, I forgot the exact words!

FRANZ

So, get off the hot seat – you're a saboteur!

WAYNE

I will not. I haven't even begun. You won't let me
begin! He wants to flush me down the toilet. You
think that's fair?

FRANZ

Note the voice. I'm not being fair. I'm trying to work.
Go back to your seat.

WAYNE

Oh, thank you, that's great! Just because I'm not giving you some shtick about how I hated Mom, and how she was never home, and all the guys paying me off to get close to her. You wanna know all that stuff. It's B movie, I'm telling you, you shitty old bastard. You're just a fucking old crap-bag. With a small cock.

FRANZ

Thank you. At last some co-operation.

WAYNE

What do you mean? You haven't won! You think you've won? I'm standing up to you! I'm not moving! You think you can dominate me, you old crap-bag! Listen, I've got your number ... You just want to feature ... same as everyone else.

FRANZ

OK ... OK. You win.

The others laugh.

WAYNE

Oh great. Now they're all laughing. That's what you want, isn't it? I look ridiculous, and you come out on top.

FRANZ

So, play him. Play the top-dog. Play me ... play Franz.

WAYNE

Play you? (*He pulls a face.*) Jesus!

But he goes into a wicked mimicry of Franz's amble and physical gestures. The others laugh. He exaggerates. They laugh more.

WAYNE

(*In Franz's accent.*) What are you ... what do you
think you are, hanh? You want to screw with me, I'm
the beeg man around here ... you're nothing ... little
shithead ... nothing at all ... you don't exist, you're
the fucking wallpaper ... (*losing the accent*) ... I
don't even see you. You're not there. You don't exist ...

FRANZ

OK. Change seats. Play the other one.

WAYNE

Who? You mean me? The one you're trying to put ...

FRANZ

Yah.

WAYNE

Oh, very clever. You come out on top, the big wise guy,
I come out nothing ... just a pair of hands for picking
up the shoes, why should I play your game, it's not
my ... listen, I'm a star ... I have talent.

FRANZ

You're playing the top guy – you're on the wrong
script. You see? You don't co-operate.

WAYNE

(*Takes a deep breath, frowns, pauses, breathes deep
again*) OK. OK. I'm nothing ... I'm co-operating! I'm
nothing ... just the fucking leavings. Fucking dregs
in the fucking cup ... a nothing, right? That's what
you want, isn't it? Just a fucking empty hole in ... oh,
that's great ... great ...

FRANZ

What do you feel?

WAYNE

What do you think I feel? I feel nothing. I'm squashed
flat, you bitch . . . how can I . . . I can't . . . that's why I . . .

FRANZ

Tell us what you feel . . . this minute . . .

WAYNE

I don't feel anything! Get your fucking yellow teeth
out of my face, I tell you I don't . . . I can't . . . how can I
dance when I don't feel anything?

FRANZ

You feel nothing . . . at this minute?

WAYNE

No!

FRANZ

But you are trembling.

WAYNE

No . . . nothing.

FRANZ

You don't feel your arms . . . *(WAYNE shakes his
head.)* . . . your legs?

WAYNE

No. *(Pause.)* No. I can't feel my legs . . . I can't feel my
face, I can't feel my dick . . . You just fucking won't let
me exist, will you? You just want to stamp me out.

FRANZ

Change seats.

WAYNE

I can't.

FRANZ

Go on. Go on, Wayne – play the top dog again.

WAYNE

I ... It's not ... I can't find him. *(Slight pause.)* You're
nothing. A piece of shit. A big hole ... nothing ... no
right to exist ... no talent ...

FRANZ

Now say all these things again, but after each one
say: it's a lie.

WAYNE

I'm nothing ... it's a lie ... I'm a piece of shit ... it's
a ... it's a ... *(He starts to cry)* ... I do have legs ... I
do have arms ... I do have feet. *(He cries.)* I'm here. I
do have a right ... I don't know ... but I am here. I do
exist. Oh Christ. *(Cries.)*

FRANZ

Just think. You are competing so much with your
mother, the star, that you got to carry her around
with you all the time, taking a peek to make sure
she's really dead!

WAYNE cries.

FRANZ

Well, that's not so bad. *(Slight pause.)* Not so bad as
the one who's really putting you down all the time,
eh?

WAYNE cries.

WAYNE

(Through his tears.) You don't know how tough it is.

FRANZ

So why compete with yourself all the time? (*Pause.*)
That's what you're doing.

WAYNE

I have to be self-critical – judge myself, in order to …

FRANZ

Not at all. (*Slight pause, WAYNE sniffs.*) You mean,
to discover new things? New ways to express your
talent? You got to nitpick, be a carrion eater of
yourself? No wonder you don't want to get up in the
morning. No wonder you don't feel your legs … you
got a bloody enemy waiting there for you. Not even
with a nice cup of coffee! 'Come on, Wayne, wake
up so that I can start beating you into the ground,
you nothing' … 'I think I stay in bed, I don't feel so
good …'

WAYNE'S shoulders droop. He sits, miserable.

FRANZ

Don't worry … don't worry, kid … don't think to find
it easy. The journey proceeds. When you confront, you
find you manage … the fear disperses …

WAYNE recovers slightly, lifts his head. PAULA makes to give him
a Kleenex, but FRANZ waves her back.

PAULA

(*Not to be denied.*) You're a great dancer, Wayne.

FRANZ

(*Gently.*) No, don't praise him. Doesn't help. Already
he depends too much on the opinion of others.

They wait. WAYNE clears his throat.

WAYNE

She was a lousy mother. I didn't love her. *(Pause.)* I liked her. Very good legs.

FRANZ

Good. That disposes of Mother.

WAYNE

She never really made it.

FRANZ

Doesn't follow that you won't. Of course, if you keep sabotaging – maybe you do it to disappoint her for neglecting you and not getting you a father? Anyway, being such a good son, the shit has to go someplace.

WAYNE

I'm not good.

FRANZ

He thinks he's bad – even more arrogant.

WAYNE

(Sarcastic.) Thank you.

CHRIS

What's wrong with dependence? Plenty of parasites in nature.

FRANZ

Ah, the genetic biologist!

CHRIS

Dependence is very efficient.

FRANZ

(Growls.) Not against fascism it ain't.

CHRIS

I'm not talking about politics ...

FRANZ

Politics is people, and if we don't evolve from carnivorous predators pretty soon, we're going to be extinct!

CHRIS

What do you suggest?

FRANZ

(Tired, he doesn't want to get into this.) That we evolve from imperialism.

PAULA

Huh?

FRANZ

... from systems designed to protect the strong from the weak ... from training our children to maintain this system by proffering love only as reward for good behaviour, thus creating races of automata with murderous tendencies ... *(His energy seems to have dissolved.)*

CHRIS

(Slight pause.) How you going to fix all that?

FRANZ

I'm not, you are.

CHRIS

You kidding?

FRANZ

Darling, you got just the qualities for it, you're a romantic, thank God. *(This puts CHRIS totally out of face.)* I've seen you with the plants, taking care of things. No ... *(He pauses, a long pause, thinking.)* Our parents don't own us. Neither does the state ... nor God, for if everything is determined and we're just puppets what the fuck is anything for? No. Better we develop our own support systems – you never know when you're going to need them. Keep in trim ... the mind ... the heart ... the soul, as well as the body. You have to live with yourself, so it's better to like it, accept ourselves, as we are – let's face it, we can never fulfil the hopes of others. If we are a failure they are outraged – even worse if we are a success, then the green eye. And no good playing the regular guy, there are degrees of regular. Did I tell you the story of the rabbi? The rabbi stands before the congregation and says, Lord, I'm a fine rabbi, but I am nothing. Then the cantor, he steps forward and he says ... Lord, I'm a very fine singer, but I too am nothing. Notice he pauses a little bit longer than the rabbi ... he's an upstager. And a little guy gets up from the congregation and says, Lord, I'm not such a bad tailor, but I too am nothing. And the rabbi looks at the cantor, and the cantor looks at the rabbi and says: Who does he think he is to think he's nothing? It's not your mother ... your father ... the cold-water apartment on the seventh floor without elevator. It's not your sex ... it's not your nationality ... your colour. All here. *(He touches his head.)* Here. We are our own battlefields. We believe that we see things straight – that we have perspective. But it is our perspective. From our eyes only. Maybe a Martian sees light as pink champagne. Maybe, to an ant, a fava bean is a geodesic dome. Who knows? As Albert Einstein has told us … I knew him well, by the way … never was able to beat me at chess, no head for figures … *(They laugh)* … the world exists only for us because only we see it. It's all ours! When you got it, flaunt it … but do we? Do we hell! How can we properly fulfil ourselves when we constantly permit ourselves to be regulated by outside pressure? The kittens learn from the cat, but do they want to fulfil Mom's ambitions? And what about Mommy? Does she exist solely for my tabby son the lawyer, my ginger son the famous doctor? Are you kidding? The mommy cat is out screwing someplace. She has other things on her mind. *(To WAYNE.)* I like your mother, she sounds a real woman. Once we project some part of our potential then this potential turns against us.

PAULA

I don't understand. What do you mean?

FRANZ

Once we live only through the eyes of others, we don't see, we are only seen. We don't hear, we exist only to be overheard. We see ourselves as an imagined sum of the judgements of others. And thus, we become automata. We become rigid. We become phobic. We become paranoid. We are invalids. Needing attention. Only when we reject the demands from without, becoming as it seems – but only seems – selfish … only then can we truly consult ourselves, discover, with open minds, what it is that we need. And then, abracadabra, what it is that we can contribute. It may be something more risky – or something entirely less

grandiose than we expected, or was expected from
us by others. But surprise is refreshing. A shower of
rain, beautiful. We are, you see, directional. As plants
are. A tulip becomes a tulip, a dahlia, a dahlia. So we,
too, must become people, turning towards the light . . .
open . . . alert . . . curious . . . ready . . . and alive. And
now I must stop hypnotising you. Thank you. We
worked well today . . . you helped me, and I gave you
my wisdom. Now I go to make myself pretty. I hope
you all got nice presents for me. I am a greedy man.

PAULA

You said gifts were consolations!

FRANZ

So, console me! And don't listen to anything I say. I
see you all tonight.

He goes. The others leave severally. Pause. Light change. Scramble
of sounds on the P/A.

P/A

Norman Levy . . . Norman Levy please . . . you're wanted
in reception. Could somebody move the truck in the
garbage area please . . . could you remove the blue Chevy
truck in the garbage area, you're blocking the driveway.

Loud burst as the P/A is switched on. Mess of sound as adjustment
is made.

The stage darkens.

P/A

(*Urgent.*) Coral . . . could we have Coral, please, to the
lower patio?

One after the other, the banks of fairy lights come on, and the
Chinese lanterns. The effect is magical. Pause.

PAULA enters. She is wearing a red bikini decorated with small pieces of black fur. She has a large black fur tail and fur cat ears. She teeters on high heels, putting down a tray of goodies in order to blow up large blue balloons.

APRIL enters. She is wearing a soft, silky dress, and makeup. She looks comely.

> PAULA

Hi.

> APRIL

(*Jumps slightly.*) Oh! Hullo ... (*She looks round at the decorations.*) Oh, it's lovely!

> PAULA

You wanna try one of my patties?

> APRIL

Thanks.

> PAULA

They're really good ... strawberry and tuna fish ...

APRIL'S hand is arrested in midair.

> PAULA

No, go ahead ... try one.

She takes one herself and chews thoughtfully.

> PAULA

Original, huh? (*APRIL'S smile is wan.*)

She gives APRIL a hefty drink. APRIL drinks, likes it, and drinks some more.

> APRIL

This is rather tasty.

PAULA

My special brew.

She refills APRIL'S glass, then cranes dangerously, affixing balloons.

APRIL

(*As the drink rises to her head*) Whoo!

She looks up, watching PAULA work.

PAULA

(*Head in the palms.*) What's your problem?

APRIL

Beg pardon?

PAULA

What are you here for?

APRIL

I'm here with a friend.

PAULA

Aw, come on.

APRIL

No, really.

PAULA

OK. Is he getting any help?

APRIL

It's a woman.

PAULA

(*Cheerfully.*) Gay, huh?

APRIL

No, no! That is ... I've nothing ... I'm sure it must be ...
(*slightly out of her depth*) ... fun. If you ... you know ...

PAULA

Sure. What's your friend's problem?

APRIL

I'm here with Miss Valentine.

PAULA

Wow, really? I saw her in the solarium – listen, there's
something I'd like to know. Are those her own …

APRIL

Yes. And no, she hasn't had surgery.

PAULA

They're beautiful. I have a real thing about breasts.
Maybe because my mother gave me formula – were
you formula fed?

APRIL

Oh, well … I don't know … I can't remember!

They laugh.

PAULA

I'm going to do it. Feed my baby. To hell with the sag.
You can always get a couple of tucks after.

APRIL

(The nurse speaking.) Oh yes, it's so much better for
baby. Are you expecting … are you pregnant?

PAULA

Hell no. Why, are you?

APRIL

Heavens no. (She grimaces. A pause.)

She moves away, restless, and then returns to watch. She hands
PAULA a balloon, and watches her tie it.

PAULA

(*Looks down.*) Why'd you quit the session? You really threw the old guy.

APRIL

Oh dear, I didn't mean to.

PAULA

He gets nervous.

APRIL

The Professor? You do surprise me. (*Slight pause.*) Tell me ... is ... I mean, is the work here recognised? I mean, can you be referred by your doctor?

PAULA

Watcha mean? You pay your money, you choose. It's your life. People go by results.

APRIL

I wouldn't have thought humiliating people was a good way to get ...

PAULA

Oh, don't pay any attention to Franz ...

APRIL

But he's so rude!

PAULA

Yeah, but never unintentionally, huh? (*Laughs.*)

APRIL

He does seem able to lay on the charm when he wants.

PAULA

Horny old bastard. Hey, you wanna watch me dance? Come on!

APRIL follows her off, pausing to affix two balloons.

Slight pause. MAX appears, in a white tuxedo. He loses his nerve, goes back the way he came.

On the P/A, sounds of party … laughter, glasses, a chorus of 'Happy Birthday' followed by cheers. During this, MAX walks determinedly across the stage towards the sound, his present clutched in both hands.

The sound of a Viennese waltz, elegiac.

Loud applause and whistles. The music up again, and WAYNE dances on. PAULA and FRANZ follow, arm in arm, and sit to watch him dance. As the music ends he collapses stylishly on the cushions. They applaud.

PAULA

Wayne, you're fantastic.

FRANZ

My boy, you're a fine artist.

WAYNE

(*Breathless.*) I know that. (*Goes.*)

PAULA

You helped him.

FRANZ

Nah, nah. Not my affair.

PAULA

Monster. (*She kisses him lightly, pulling his beard.*)

FRANZ

Be careful, I'm a dirty old man.

PAULA

And I'm a dirty young girl – hey, you know what I'm gonna give you for your birthday? (*She whispers in his ear and screeches with laughter.*)

FRANZ

(*Wincing.*) Listen – listen, Paula, you want to do me a favour?

PAULA

Anything, Master, I'm off the hook tonight!

FRANZ

Be a little bit nice to Max for me.

PAULA

Sure, why not, how far you want me to go?

FRANZ

I think he is ready for maybe a little gentle flirtation. A couple of drinks … (*He waggles his hand.*)

PAULA

(*Sing-song.*) I get your dri-hift!

FRANZ

But Paula … Paula, listen, whatever you do, don't seduce him, that's going to terrify him, you know? And don't talk dirty.

She peals with laughter, climbs off him and goes.

FRANZ walks about, looks at his watch, smooths his head.

APRIL appears.

FRANZ

Ach. I was looking for you.

APRIL

They needed a hand in the bar.

FRANZ

Let me see. *(He inspects her soberly.)* Very nice.

APRIL

It's too formal, I'm afraid.

FRANZ

Not at all, very nice. May I get you a drink? *(He pours wine.)* We grow it here, it's very good.

They sip formally. Then he puts down his glass, takes hers and puts it aside and makes a sudden dive up her skirt, his head disappearing. She gives a loud shriek of alarm.

APRIL

What are you doing? No, please ... ah! ... what are you doing! Oh ... ah! Professor Muller, stop it ... stop it, please ... !

He throws her flat on her back on the seat, whips off her knickers and tosses them over his shoulder, dives under again.

APRIL

No! ... Please ... what are you doing?

CHRIS enters.

CHRIS

Franz, are you ready to judge the tango?

APRIL, horribly, embarrassed, tries to pull down her skirt, turning her head away from CHRIS to hide her identity.

CHRIS

Franz ... Franz? You wanna take a look at the tango?

A muffled reply from FRANZ. APRIL, helplessly, pinned, grimaces
up at CHRIS with a little social smile.

> APRIL

Look, could you go away?

> CHRIS

What do you want me to do? They're waiting!

FRANZ emerges, highly irritable.

> FRANZ

For God's sake, my boy, what do you want? You want
to spoil this lady's orgasm, is that what you want?

This is too much for APRIL. She jumps up, evading FRANZ. Since
FRANZ is being so ratty, CHRIS appeals to her.

> CHRIS

Look, how long d'you want? I'll tell them to hold it
up ... how long you going to be?

But APRIL hops away, trying to put on her knickers.

> FRANZ

(Roars) Get Out!!!

> CHRIS

(Highly irritable) What's the matter with you?
(He stumps off irritably.)

> FRANZ

(To APRIL.) April, what you doing, what you doing?
Aw, come on ... come on ...

> APRIL

I'm just ... *(pulling away from him unsuccessfully.)*
I'm just ... Look, would you let go of my knickers,
please, I really think this farce has ...

He leaps on her.

> APRIL

Get out! Get Off me!

They pull at the knickers and she is swung round. He lets go, and she tries to evade him across the seat.

> APRIL

(Very ruffled, managing to get possession of her knickers at last.) Now that's enough!

> FRANZ

Whatsamatter? Whatsamatter?

> APRIL

This is too bloody much! Honestly!

> FRANZ

Bloody much, bloody much … we got nothing yet … what are you talking about?

> APRIL

I see. What do you want – a performance? Give them a turn on the floor?

> FRANZ

Oh, come on … April … come on …

> APRIL

He'll be having a wonderful time in there, telling all his friends …

> FRANZ

So what? Who cares? The poor bastard hasn't got any friends … you should be nice to him … and to me.

> APRIL

Why should I?

FRANZ

You know why. Come ... no, come please ... look, we
take our drinks ... no, please ... it will be nice ... you
like me. Why don't you look at me? Come ... nobody
will see us. (*He persuades her to a space upstage left
where there are palms in pots*) ... then you can look
at me, we can talk and nobody will see us ... we have
a drink ... (*By this time, he has got her down on the
beach mattress under the palms.*) We have our drinks
later ...

He lies on top of her and APRIL'S knickers come flying over the
foliage.

FRANZ

Oh my God ... my God! ...

APRIL

What is it, what's the matter?

FRANZ

(*Very excited.*) You are wearing brasseer ... a
brasseer ... you are wearing brasseer – no, no, don't
take it off ... Please ... please keep it on for me ... oh
my God, it's going to be all right ... April, April ... oh
mein Gott ... you smell so good ... be a nice girl for me,
I'm going to do it, no question, you are a brilliant girl, a
brilliant girl ... oh, your smell ... what is this smell ... ?

APRIL

Yardleys.

FRANZ

(*Groaning with delight*) Yardleys! Oh ... so beautiful!
(*He begins to grunt and pant.*) Beautiful ... oh, oh,
oh ... what a delight for me ... you are so pale, my
darling ... like a peeled almond ... your skin is

gleaming – oh, oh … oh, oh, oh … oh, say something
to me, in mein ear, say something dirty for me …
quick, quick, quick …

> APRIL

Shut up, I'm trying to concentrate … I could kill you I
could kill you I could kill you … oh!!

> FRANZ

You came already?

> APRIL

Oh … oh … all right you wicked old sod. What do
you want? I'll tell you what you are – you're a dirty,
wicked old man. I know what you want, you want me
dirty, dirty, dirty … but I won't, I won't, I won't!

He grunts passionately.

> FRANZ

Oh! Ah! We came together …

They breathe deeply, gasping, getting their breath back.

> FRANZ

Oh, mein Gott. You got a bite inside you, you know
that, liebling?

> APRIL

(*Giggles*) I thought you were going to throttle me.

> FRANZ

I didn't hurt you?

> APRIL

No, no.

> FRANZ

Really?

APRIL

No, no, no.

Silence. They doze.

MAX enters, clutching a script. Walking across nervously, he comes across April's knickers. He looks down at them, transfixed. He looks about, to make sure that he is not observed, picks them up, looks round again, just manages, with a leap of fright, to stuff them in his pocket as PAULA appears.

PAULA

What you doing?

He stands, gibbering in terror, unable to reply.

PAULA

Hey, I liked your act!

MAX

(Stammers.) Thenk you. (He manages a stiff little bow.)

PAULA

No, I mean it. Needs more pace – you know? ... but once or twice you really hit the spot!

MAX

You think so?

PAULA

I know so. (She loops her forefinger into the front of his trousers and begins to pull him towards the exit.) I really understood what you were trying to say, Max ... you know, you have a truly tender imagination, that is so rare in a man ...

MAX

(Groans) Ohhh ...

PAULA

Why don't we go down by the lake? (*She manhandles
him off.*)

A slight pause.

FRANZ

Darling . . .

APRIL

What?

FRANZ

I can't breathe.

She climbs off him.

FRANZ

(*As she does so*) Ooh . . . ah . . . ah . . . ah!

APRIL

(*Kneeling up.*) Oh, I think the skirt's gone. It's my
Jean Muir dress.

FRANZ

And you kept it on for me. You don't know what this
means . . . this rustle, whisper of silk . . .

APRIL

It's rayon.

FRANZ

No matter . . . so soft . . . shining . . .

She moves apart, crosses to table, finds paper tissues, wipes herself
fastidiously, cleans up. She looks for her knickers but cannot find
them. FRANZ suddenly barks with laughter, making her laugh.

APRIL

What's the matter?

FRANZ

I was thinking of old Schoenfeld. I used to go to his
seminars, when I was working for my doctorate.
Heinrich Schoenfeld, disciple of Freud, but not
uncritical. Very strict man ... you know, stiff collar,
pince nez ... always the spats, the umbrella, the
Homburg hat. One day we were dozing through his
seminars as usual when he says suddenly, in that
Bavarian accent of his "You can never fuck enough."
"Fuck." ... "Geshrecht" ... just like that! We all, you
know – (*He sits up rigidly, his eyes wide, then laughs*).
We listened for two whole terms after but he never
says another rude word. We begin to think were we
dreaming? I have wondered so many times – what
made him say it?

APRIL

Perhaps it's true.

FRANZ

Oh yah, sure! But Schoenfeld? And if he knew that ... !

He gets up heavily, crosses to seat, wincing slightly as he sits, then
making himself comfortable with cushions.

APRIL

What's the matter?

FRANZ

Arthritis in mein hip.

She finishes combing her hair and comes and sits beside him. And
combs his beard.

APRIL

You look like a Greek Colonel.

FRANZ

More like a Hamburg pork butcher.

APRIL

Not at all. *(Pouring drinks for them.)*

FRANZ

Ilse says so.

APRIL

(Arrested, drink in hand.) Oh dear. How on earth am I going to look her in the face? Your wife?

FRANZ

(Surprised.) Ilse? Ach, don't worry. She is not concerned. Our little affair will not incommode. It's not important to her. Anyway, believe me, she hates messy women.

APRIL

I see.

FRANZ

Hey, I don't say it's not important to me, April. I am not some plausible flirt. I am in love with you. Doesn't that make you happy?

APRIL

Oh, come on.

FRANZ

How can you doubt it? We have just proved our love ... I would have proved it twice, maybe – only you winded me little bit ...

APRIL

(Amused.) Twice!

FRANZ

(*Pursues his advantage.*) Twice! Three times ...
four ... five ... why not? We are alive!

He embraces her. She draws back after, smiling. But catches him
giving her a shrewd, objective look. She jerks away abruptly.

FRANZ

What's the matter?

APRIL

Nothing.

FRANZ

No, no ... come on ... what is it?

APRIL

It's nothing. (*But he shakes her arm.*) Why did you
look at me like that?

FRANZ

Like what?

APRIL

I'm not a fool, you know.

FRANZ

What are you talking about? ...

APRIL

Please stop it, Professor.

FRANZ

If I look at you it's because ...

APRIL

Oh don't!

FRANZ

Why can't I look at you? What's wrong?

APRIL

You looked at me like something under a microscope.

Slight pause.

FRANZ

I ... wanted to see if you are happy ... if I had pleased
you.

APRIL

Oh rats.

FRANZ

Not at all, not at all. A man is never sure. Women ...
dissemble. And, yah ... I am doctor too ... it is my
nature. I wish to observe our little experiment.

APRIL

I see. An experiment.

FRANZ

A very nice one.

APRIL

All part of the treatment here, no doubt ... every
inmate guaranteed a quick screw. Is it in the
brochure? If I were you, I'd be a bit more careful. One
of these days somebody's going to – well, I'd hardly
call it ethical.

FRANZ

Oh! Hoho! You think I take advantage of you? You
think I break my Hippocratic oath? My God, if you
think I risk my career ... my reputation for you,
April ... you should be very flattered, that a man
would take this risk for you. Look, don't bully me.
I have no more status here than you. Reputation,
maybe, status, no. You come as you are – no paper

credentials. Here we are responsible for ourselves
and to, but not for one another, so don't insult me with
these cheap threats. I love you, isn't that enough?
Doesn't it please you? It should, I am an important
man.

APRIL

An experiment. You said so yourself.

FRANZ

I am greedy! I wanted to see what you were feeling,
that maybe, maybe I had gratified you. And yes, of
course, naturally I don't want that you make a fool of
yourself, that wouldn't be convenient for either of us.

APRIL

You see? You're a cruel man.

FRANZ

April, why should I give you crap? I may drop dead
tomorrow. Yes, I withdraw from you – you find that
irresponsible? Why be depressed? We can't make
love all night. At least I can't. I don't know about
you.

APRIL

Bloody men! As soon as they get what they want they
can't wait to be out of the door. A couple of days and
you wouldn't know me in the street!

FRANZ

No, no, no … Longer than that! But OK, maybe not,
after a while. I am a busy man. I meet so many people.
I'm famous now. I don't have time to remember.

APRIL

Get it while you can.

FRANZ

Yes! Yes!

APRIL

It's all so self-centered!

FRANZ

While you think only of others.

APRIL

Somebody has to.

FRANZ

Keeps you busy.

APRIL

Better than all this wallowing.

FRANZ

Oh yah. And better than looking at the holes in your own personality. But we have to look at them. We see them. Loving sister, dutiful daughter who wishes only to help us, but we can't help you. Oh no, that's not permitted. Perhaps we, too, need to stroke someone? But you don't want to be stroked ... only I know different. *(Pulls her cruelly by the hair.)* I found out! Didn't I?

APRIL

(Pulls away.) If you're going to be destructive, I'm off!

FRANZ

Sit down! Can't you see? This is where he was wrong!

APRIL

Who?

FRANZ

Freud ... Freud! He thought a person would not
mature because of a childhood trauma. It's the
other way round! I never yet listened to one of these
kiddies' traumas that wasn't a lie! We cling to lies!
Lies! Anything to justify our unwillingness to grow
up. To leave such cosy prisons of invented memory,
to be responsible for our own lives, to make ourselves
up, existentially, day by day, knowing that we, and
only we create the world. My God! Such courage
we need! Who would want to be mature? Rebirth?
Satori? The coming to the senses? No thank you,
not for me please. Let me stay in the trance and
masturbate! April, I tell you, we are the Living
Dead, most of us – Zombies! Ah ha ha ha ha! To force
ourselves awake? To take control? I tell you – not so
easy. Listen my dear, you renew me. And I know that I
please you, fascinate you little bit. I see it in your face.
Isn't that something? Isn't that enough? I want us to
be mutual. Whether we meet or not ... to be friends ...
whether we make love or not ... to be friends. But not
to possess, exclusive ...

APRIL

Oh, it's fine for you.

FRANZ

What do you mean! I am old! What do you want? That
I become obsessed with you? Go round with a carving
knife every time I see you talking with a young man?
I know all about jealousy, believe me.

APRIL

Well, anyway, I daresay you've more than enough
handmaidens ready to make a fuss of you.

FRANZ

You want to join them? Sit in the sun, become the
guardian of the great man, of the shrine. Is that what
you want?

APRIL

I don't know. I daresay I could make myself useful.

FRANZ

Oh yah. And wouldn't you do it well, my dear,
writing up the notes, so unselfish, never answering
back when I shout, so they all pity you – totally
indispensable – and evaporating completely into
Franz. Do you know what I say to that? I say – get off!
Get off me! Get off my back and stop choking me – I
can't breathe!

APRIL

I haven't said a word! What are you talking about? I
don't want anything from you, it's ridiculous!

FRANZ

Can I give you marriage, children? It's what you
want!

APRIL

Nothing of the sort!

FRANZ

I'm telling you, if you stay here to stroke Franz
for the last years of his life, you'll be past it. I am a
beautiful, attractive man, but a little old for you. You
need a young man of forty to father your kids.

APRIL

If I get any.

FRANZ

Your mother managed, poor, deprived lady you so
want to be like. She even managed to sing! April,
when we are small, those around us force a shape
on us to suit themselves. We have to find ourselves
again, re-inhabit the city. We have to take charge.

APRIL

I think I'm perfectly capable of that.

FRANZ

No, no. Not with discipline, force – with love,
imagination! Discover … create your own life. Create
circumstance for it to happen. Insist. Only by making
appropriate demands can we be truly unselfish.

APRIL

Nonsense, we have to deny ourselves, otherwise we'd
be monsters.

FRANZ

Does a tree deny itself? Does a cloud? A cloud is
not selfish. It seeks only its place – not the place of
others, nor more than one place. It lives … here …
now. If you think that by sitting very still, hoping
that nothing will come and eat you. If you think that,
by this, you make no demands, you are mistaken.
You demand enormously. We all have to find our
Kingdoms. Do you want to be like the boy Kay – with
splinters of ice in his heart? Like the Snow Queen?

He crosses to her, bends over, and shouts, very loud, into her face.

FRANZ

Wake up!!!

Then he kisses her tenderly.

FRANZ

I ... your Prince Charming ... kiss you awake.

Despite herself, she smiles up at him, entranced. He takes her hand.

FRANZ

April, those around us are not houses to be lived in, meals to be eaten. But neither are they fearful forests ... deadly swamps, and nor ... and this is most important for you ... nor are they some race of gods and goddesses with access and rights to some privileged existence from which you are both unqualified and forever exiled. To live free, you must – ach! *(He strikes himself heavily on the chest.)*

APRIL

(Alarmed) What's the matter?

FRANZ

Must ... Should ... I am telling you what to do. I am giving you solutions, the thing I most hate! *(He kisses her hand.)* Don't listen to Franz. Listen to yourself – listen to April. Let April speak. Only you can make your life. Only you.

APRIL

You make it sound as if we're all on our own.

FRANZ

Well, aren't we? We arrive alone, we leave alone. A little participation in between. When we face this,

that there is no insurance, then we can enjoy our
lives, no? A bit of heart ... that's all ... ...

He suddenly seems very tired, and old. A long pause.

> FRANZ

God, I could eat a buffalo. I'm hungry!

> APRIL

I'll get you something.

But she sits, thoughtful, playing with the skirt of her dress.

> APRIL

Yes, but ...

> FRANZ

Forget the buts ... forget the buts ...

> APRIL

Oh! *(She gets up.)* What do you feel like?

> FRANZ

Anything. A lot.

APRIL goes. PAULA enters, in merry mood.

> PAULA

Here I come, ready or no!

> FRANZ

Oh, my God.

> PAULA

What's the matter, don't you feel in the mood? Listen,
I promised, and you're gonna get it!

> FRANZ

What about? Why don't you go find Max?

PAULA

I already did.

FRANZ

Yah? How was it?

PAULA

I blew it. He thinks we're engaged.

FRANZ

You mean you seduced him? But I told you not to!

PAULA

Yeah, well you know how it is ... look, let's forget ...

FRANZ

My God, I'm going to have to listen to him for days,
and he's so boring!

PAULA

I'll take your mind right off it -

FRANZ

No, Paula, please ... please darling, I'm very tired. It's
my heart, I think it's my heart ...

PAULA

I know the very thing for it ... (She begins to grope.)

FRANZ

Believe me, Paula, believe me – nothing would please
me more. Paula, this is so embarrassing for me ...

APRIL returns with a large tray piled high with food and drink for
the two of them. She stops short.

FRANZ looks up, gives her a silly little smile and a gallant wave of
the hand. PAULA lifts her head and sees the tray.

PAULA

(*Shrieks.*) Food! You managed to get near the food,
how d'you do it? You're a genius, fantastic! Here,
lemme take the tray. Boy, it's a feast! (*To FRANZ:*)
Come on, baby, this'll give you strength. (*To APRIL:*)
You got some pie, great! Here, baby … (*She ties a
napkin round FRANZ'S neck.*)

APRIL stands motionless as PAULA sets down the food, draws up a
low table, arranges the food for the three of them, getting glasses,
and pouring swiftly. She grabs a piece of pie and throws herself
down on the further side of FRANZ, offering him food.

APRIL stands.

FRANZ looks up at her and pats the vacant space beside him, his
other hand about PAULA'S waist. It is an indication of the space
rather than a positive invitation for APRIL to sit.

APRIL looks down at the space contemplatively. Then, moving
slightly stiffly, she approaches the seat and looks down at FRANZ.
He looks up at her with a neutral expression.

Slowly, delicately, arranging her skirt, APRIL sits by his side. He
puts his other arm about her as PAULA puts food into his mouth.

On the P/A, a violent burst of Hendrix.

APRIL leans forward, takes a piece of pie, puts it down again as a
thought occurs. She turns to FRANZ. He turns to her.

APRIL

Do you know something?

FRANZ

What? (*He raises his voice above the music.*) What?

APRIL

I've just thought, (*She gazes into space, picks up the
piece of pie. She turns to him, her face urgent.*)
Most people have awful lives!

PAULA

What?

FRANZ

What did you say?

The MUSIC finishes just before she speaks.

APRIL

(*Shouts.*) I said …

She modifies her voice in the sudden silence.

APRIL

I said … most people have awful lives.

She speaks as though she has made a wondrous discovery. He
turns and gazes at her. They regard each other.

FRANZ

No. (*He shakes his head … speaks, after a pause.*) We
said, if we had a daughter, Ilse and I, we would call
her Joy. I always liked that word.

APRIL

Joy? Yes. Simple and straightforward.

He smiles briefly at her reaction, leans forward, strikes his
chest.

FRANZ

And here – in here! A beautiful emotion – joy – for all –
not just the privileged but for sharing, yah?

APRIL looks at him, nods slowly.

They smile at each other, well pleased with their evening. He puts an arm around her.

PAULA looks up, and snuggles into his other side as he extends an arm.

The End.

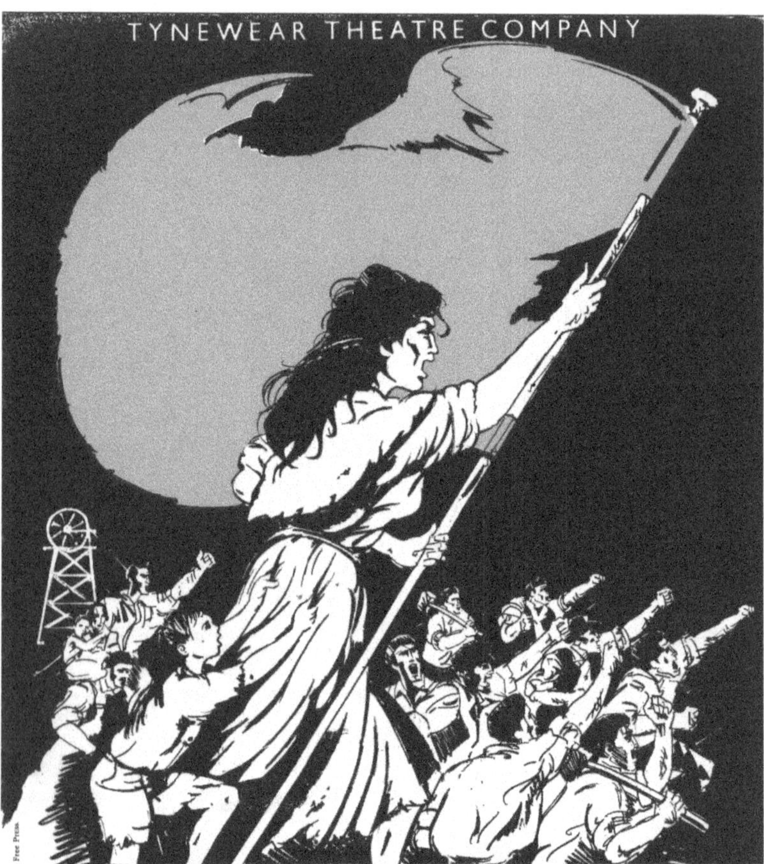

TYNEWEAR THEATRE COMPANY
IT IS BETTER TO DIE ON YOUR FEET THAN TO LIVE ON YOUR KNEES
PASIONARIA
BY PAM GEMS (Author of Piaf) LYRICS BY PAUL SAND & PAM GEMS. MUSIC BY PAUL SAND
NEWCASTLE·PLAYHOUSE
TUES 12 FEB-SAT 2 MAR MON-SAT AT 7·30 Reduced price previews 7,8,9,10,11,
(OPPOSITE HAYMARKET METRO) BARRAS BRIDGE, NEWCASTLE UPON TYNE NE1 7RH TEL (0632) 323421. 24 hrs
Design: Peter Straughan Jarvis for Harvey Straughan Jarvis. Print: Tyneside Free Press

PASIONARIA

A play with music

For Sue Dunderdale

FOREWORD

I was a child during the Spanish Civil War. There were pictures in the papers of women and children being bombed, people running, cities flattened. Spaniard fighting Spaniard – that most terrible tragedy – civil war. And reports of a woman – known as La Pasionaria – who was either a ferocious fiend, or a courageous defender of freedom, depending on the newspaper you read. Who was she? A Spanish figurehead, it seemed, famous for saying 'They shall not pass' and 'It is better to die on your feet than to live on your knees.'

Dolores Ibárruri was born in a mining community in a Spain still seemingly locked in the seventeenth century. She lived in near starvation (four of her six children were dead by the age of four). As a woman in a country dominated by the most macho culture, by oppressive Catholicism tinged with Islam, as an illiterate peasant, what hopes for her? Yet this woman became a member of Parliament in the Cortes, the Spanish government.

After Franco won the civil war, Pasionaria fled to Russia and lived in Moscow with her surviving children, Amaya and Reuben (Reuben was killed at Stalingrad). She continued to be a dynamic force, devoting herself to the lot of exiled Spaniards everywhere, and going herself to the Kremlin in 1968 to condemn the Soviet invasion of Czechoslovakia. But she longed for home.

In 1977 Franco died. Restored as the elected Deputy of Asturia, Pasionaria went to Bilbao and brought ten thousand weeping listeners to their feet, her oratory unaffected by age.

We produced "Pasionaria" in Newcastle in 1985, during the Miners' Strike, with Sue Dunderdale as director and

Denise Black as a fiery and mesmerizing Dolores. We wrote to Pasionaria for her blessing and received a video from her.

In it she said:

'I am unable to attend the performance of this work due to the circumstances in which we live. I cannot attend the performance of this play, but I wish to say that I am deeply grateful that you have taken the trouble to put on this play about the life of a working-class woman – grand-daughter, daughter and wife of miners – who has worked and been subject all her life to exploitation. It is not difficult to speak of the miners' situation, not only in our country but in all those countries where men have to survive by clawing from the earth the minerals which will enrich their exploiters.

I wish to conclude these few words by expressing my solidarity with the English miners, our fellow workers, and with their success in their struggle to improve their living conditions.'

The video showed an elderly, extremely beautiful woman, with the uniquely focused asperity of the woman politician – forever trying to juggle a personal and professional life.

Plus ça change.

Pam Gems

Pam Gems talks to Lyn Gardner about politics, people and Pasionaria – her latest play based on the life of Dolores Ibarruri, the Spanish Republican leader of the 1930s.

Whether she welcomes the prospect or not, playwright Pam Gems looks set to become the grande dame of British Theatre. She is, after all, one of that rare breed – the commercially successful woman playwright. Ms Gems stormed the West End with *Dusa, Fish Stas and Vi* (1976) and *Piaf* (The RSC success that also subsequently went to Broadway) and forced West End managers to reconsider the long-held opinion that Agatha Christie is the only woman playwright of note the theatre has produced.

There's more to Pam Gems' work than simple commercial viability; her brilliantly structured plays also provide some of the few role-models for the flourishing and increasingly vocal younger generation of female playwrights. Although she is now in her late fifties, the themes and issues apparent in her work cut across the generations and express the concerns, interests and experiences of not only older women but those who came to maturity post-1968.

Sometimes reluctant in the past to be labelled 'a feminist,' Pam Gems nevertheless reflects a post-feminist consciousness. She asks important questions: How do men and women co-exist in a changing world? Have the sexual revolution and freedom from child-bearing really liberated women? Can women find fulfilment without having children?

She came to the theatre late in life. Although her first play was written when she was eight ("the teacher cut some of the lines and I was very upset; I've since learnt that directors do it all the time") and she continued scribbling during her twenties. "I was actually more concerned with sex at the time." It was not until she moved with her family to London in the early seventies, that she began writing in earnest. 'I decided that I might as well fail doing something I enjoyed.'

She arrived in London just at the time there was a growing hunger for women's work. Her children were either almost grown up or away at school, and she was free to go to the then blossoming lunch-time theatre, and to meet with other women aspiring to write and direct. Not that it was easy: "For a woman of my age it was very difficult. I'd been very cut off. I had no connections in the theatre and suddenly I was mixing with women who had a very different style. I brought jam-puffs to meetings and they all had flat stomachs and wore jeans."

Two short plays at the Almost Free Theatre (1973) followed and led to her co-founding the Women's Theatre Company at the Roundhouse (1974.) But it was Nancy Meckler's Hampstead Theatre production of *Dusa, Fish, Stas and Vi*, which transferred to the Mayfair Theatre in 1977, that put Pam Gems firmly on the theatrical map.

Despite her recent successes at the RSC with *Piaf* and *Camille* (currently looking for a West End venue), Gems' work has not always been popular with the critics. "Writing, if your serious, is a science," says Gems. "Form is a complicated game. I don't always write in the same genre, which baffles people. They tend to want tram-lines and to know where they are with a writer but I'm not interested in writing like that."

Her latest play, *Pasionaria*, at the Newcastle Playhouse, has not been critically well-received. Based on the life of the Spanish Republican and communist leader, Dolores Ibarruri, it is an uncompromisingly political play that draws striking parallels between the recent miners' dispute and the uprising of the Asturian mining community just before the Spanish Civil War.

"Political plays," says Gems "are unfashionable. In bad times, we seem to need schlock, big musicals, and nostalgia. I'm old enough to remember a time when families were actually starving in this country. You can't turn those experiences into song-and-dance spectaculars. Modern writing seems to be more and more on a slant. We live in a decadent age and the writing is witty, elusive, and cynical. I think that is defeatist."

Pasionaria was written a few years ago, but it was rewritten to focus on the miners' strike. There can be no doubt which side Ms Gems supports: "Most people are not political so I know it's asking a lot to end the play with a long political speech. It was a calculated risk – if it isn't engaging then we have failed!"

The critics may have thought as much but as she points out "there has been such support, not just from the audience but also from the lighting people and the usherettes. It's as though we live in different countries."

But if *Pasionaria* is the first sign that a more overtly political voice is emerging, Ms Gems still intends to persist with her overwhelming concern with the relationship of women to society. "I want to write a play about feminism today. I find the need to reassess and assert for myself and to look at others to ask: Where are we now? What has been achieved over the last fifteen years, and what has been lost?"

Her interests also have a practical side. She is a founding member of the Women's Playhouse Trust – a project set up to create greater artistic opportunities and control for women in the theatre. "The lack of opportunity for women is disgraceful. It's lunatic to say that women just aren't good enough. We have many fine women directors but unless they get a chance to put on productions, they are not going to get better. It makes me despair when a man says to a woman who wants to be a lighting director "Can you lift the lights?" How does he think she lifts her three-year-old child? Younger women writers coming up are much tougher and stronger. We need them so badly. But the real danger is that they'll succumb to careerism, and just be used as tokens or played off against each other. Women must help each other if they're going to survive. That's why a project like the Women's Playhouse Trust is so important."

Pam Gems is a fine example of survival. Does she enjoy her success?

She smiles "Fame didn't do a lot for Scott Fitzgerald, did it? Pleasure for me is sitting at a desk writing, or being in the theatre at that marvellous moment when a play hits form. I can't really believe my luck that I'm in a clean, dry job that I want to do."

LYN GARDNER. City Limits. 01/03/1985

PASIONARIA was first presented at Newcastle Playhouse on the 12th of February 1985, directed by SUE DUNDERDALE, with the following cast:

DENISE BLACK	La Pasionaria
SHAY GORMAN	Dolores' father – Miner – Jesus
DANIEL HILL	Dolores' husband – Soldier – Miner – Prisoner
JUDY HOPTON	Emilia – Senora Lopez – Woman Governor – Prisoner
RICHARD CORDERY	Mine Manager – Prison Governor – Luis – Prisoner – Fernandez
MARY SHEEN	Bonifacio's Mother – Juanita – Manuela – Montalban – Prisoner
RICHARD ALBRECHT	Senor Lopez – Union Man – Manuel – Soldier – Mayor – Prime Minister
KATE McKENZIE	Dona Sebastiana – Pilar – Dancer – Secretary
LUCIEN TAYLOR	Bonifacio – José – Soldier – Civil Guard Deputy
JOSIE LAWRENCE	Luisa – Nun
BARBARA & STEPHEN HOAR EMMA & JAMES TAYLOR	La Pasionaria's children

Designed by	ALEXANDRA BYRNE
Lighting by	RAY RENNIE
Music and lyrics by	PAUL SAND
Musicians	BRUCE ARTHUR
	FRANCIS CHRISTOU
	CHRIS GLASSFIELD
Spanish Consultant	PATRICIA ROBERTS

PASIONARIA

CAST

EMILIA

DOLORES

FATHER

BONIFACIO

MOTHER

SENORA LOPEZ

SENOR LOPEZ

MINER (DOLORES' HUSBAND)

MINE MANAGER

UNION MAN

DONA SEBASTIANA

MALE PRISON GOVERNOR

SECRETARY

LUISA

NUN

PILAR

MANUELA

WOMAN PRISON GOVERNOR

LUIS

JOSÉ

MANUEL

JESUS

FIRST SOLDIER ... JUAN

SECOND SOLDIER ... PACO

MAYOR

PRIME MINISTER

MONTALBAN

FERNANDEZ

MINERS

PRISONERS

POLICE

PASIONARIA

ACT ONE

<u>ACT ONE – SCENE ONE</u>

A dark stage. Silence.

Then the urgent, repeated sound of a hooter.
MUSIC with percussion comes in over this. The Music reduces to
a single drum.

A slow parade of WOMEN and MEN cross the back of the stage. They
are in mourning, some carry small posies of flowers.
They go.

EMILIA enters with a newspaper.

> EMILIA
>
> (*Reads:*) 'The end of the Franco regime has meant,
> after thirty-eight years of exile, the return to Spain
> of Dolores Ibárruri. Arriving on the 13th of May
> 1977, she has resumed her seat in the Spanish
> Parliament as Deputy of the Asturias region. On
> May 22nd, in Bilbao, Dolores Ibárruri, her legendary
> powers of oration undimmed by her eighty-one years,
> brings 10,000 cheering and weeping listeners to their
> feet. La Pasionaria has returned to Spain.' Dolores
> Ibárruri. La Pasionaria. A peasant woman ... born
> in the cold, wet north of Spain. Grand-daughter,
> daughter ... and wife, of a miner. The time? The
> twenties, thirties – though you'd hardly believe it,
> most of Spain seems lost somewhere in the 16th

century. Life expectancy for most people? Forty –
with luck. Worse for women, with pregnancies,
haemorrhages, infection, a repressive Catholicism,
and the lingering influence of Islam. But not much
chance for anyone.

She goes as a MAN enters separately.

ACT ONE – SCENE TWO

The MAN, painfully crippled, sweeps the streets. His lurching
actions are counterpointed by the MUSIC of a pipe which seems
to mock him.

A YOUNG WOMAN in cap and apron, and wearing clogs enters,
books in hand. She watches the MAN, unseen.

> DOLORES
>
> *(As the MAN bends once more,)* Leave it. *(She laughs.)*
> You're paid by the hour, not the job.

> FATHER
>
> Those books of yours are making you dishonest.

> DOLORES
>
> You shouldn't be sweeping the streets. You're a face-
> worker. They should give you something decent.

> FATHER
>
> I'm lucky to get . . .

> DOLORES
>
> Lucky?

She grabs the broom as he makes to pick it up again. He gives her
a clout over the head, without rancour, which sends her reeling.

FATHER

Watch your mouth, Dolores. And keep away from that
library. You'll be losing your own place next.

DOLORES

(A wail, watching him stoop.) Dad!

FATHER

It's better than being idle ... Oh, hullo young Bon.

A YOUNG LAD of fragile appearance enters, a small coffin under
his arm.

FATHER

Where you off to?

DOLORES

(Sour.) What you got there? (Together)

BONIFACIO

Me sister.

DOLORES

(Protest.) Oh, not the littl'un with the fair hair? Ah,
what a shame, what a shame.

BONIFACIO

Wanna look?

She shakes her head, and sees that this hurts his feelings.

DOLORES

Oh, all right.

DOLORES and her FATHER look in the coffin, her FATHER taking
off his cap.

FATHER

Any word from the board? About your Dad?

BONIFACIO

Yeah.

DOLORES

Oh, what?

BONIFACIO

We got a letter. (*He is proud of this.*)

FATHER

How much? Full pension? (*The BOY shakes his head.*)
Lump sum? (*But the BOY just looks at him.*)

DOLORES

(*Harsh.*) How much?

BONIFACIO

(*Mutters, humiliated.*) Nothing.

DOLORES

Nothing?

FATHER

Nothing?

DOLORES

What do you mean, nothing?

BONIFACIO

Dad was doing a shift for a mate. As a favour. They
say it don't count.

DOLORES

(*Apart, with a frightening grin.*) Getting killed don't
count? Leaving six kids don't count?

BONIFACIO

Five.

DOLORES

What?

BONIFACIO

(Juggling the coffin.) Five now.

DOLORES

Oh. Yeah. Here.

She holds out her arms, and takes the coffin. The FATHER puts his hand in his pocket, takes out a coin, looks at it, and gives it to the BOY.

FATHER

For your mother.

BONIFACIO

Thanks! *(Runs off quickly.)*

DOLORES glares at her FATHER.

DOLORES

How much did you give him!

DOLORES leaves with BABY'S coffin. Her FATHER sweeps, and goes.

Fade to black.

ACT ONE – SCENE THREE

A poor interior.

A WOMAN sits motionless before an empty grate.

DOLORES and BONIFACIO enter, each holding one end of the coffin. The WOMAN looks up briefly. Where to put the coffin? They put it on the table, but DOLORES feels this inappropriate. She upends the coffin and leans it against the table leg.

> BONIFACIO
>
> (*Hisses.*) Not that one!

> DOLORES
>
> Why not?

> BONIFACIO
>
> It's where the cat scratches.

DOLORES pulls a face, and moves the coffin to another table leg. BONIFACIO crosses, sidles up to his MOTHER, who continues to stare into the empty grate. He puts the coin on the corner of the table nearest to her.

> BONIFACIO
>
> It's from Dolores' Dad.

His MOTHER looks up at him slowly. Everything she does is as if under water. She looks at the coin, and then at DOLORES. She shakes her head to DOLORES.

> DOLORES
>
> It's for you.

The MOTHER looks at the coin.

> MOTHER
>
> (*Slight pause, she speaks with difficulty.*) Thank your father, Dolores.

She looks up at DOLORES. DOLORES stands over her, staring down at her, almost a glare.

> BONIFACIO
>
> Do you want a drink of water?

Silence.

BONIFACIO

(*To DOLORES, at last.*) Hey ... I'm leaving!

DOLORES

School?

BONIFACIO

Yeah!

DOLORES

When?

BONIFACIO

Next week! I got a job!

A hush.

MOTHER

Job? What job?

BONIFACIO

I got a job, Mum.

MOTHER

What job? What's that ... in your hand?

BONIFACIO

It's Dad's cap.

MOTHER

Put it away.

BONIFACIO

Look, it fits me!

MOTHER

Take it off. Put it away, I tell you.

BONIFACIO

I'm the man of the house now.

But he takes off the cap, and screws it between his hands.

> BONIFACIO
>
> I went down the mine office.

> MOTHER
>
> No.

> BONIFACIO
>
> They let me sign on.

> MOTHER
>
> You're not going. You're not old enough.

> BONIFACIO
>
> I'm eleven!

> MOTHER
>
> I'll go down the school.

> BONIFACIO
>
> I've already signed.

> MOTHER
>
> No!! With your father not rotted in his shroud yet?
> I'll crush your feet first.

> BONIFACIO
>
> I'm the man of the house now.

> MOTHER
>
> Is that what you want? Never see daylight, cough up
> your lungs when you're forty, if they haven't crushed
> your back ...

Silence. She sits looking at the fire, as before.

BONIFACIO, embarrassed, fidgets, kicking a foot against a chair
maddeningly.

DOLORES prowls at a distance. She sidles along the table and picks up a fearsome knife, whetted to narrowness above its old bone handle. She begins to tap-tap with it, looking covertly at the MOTHER several times.

BONIFACIO clears his throat.

> BONIFACIO
>
> Did they come? (*His MOTHER looks up at him.*)

> DOLORES
>
> The women from the Church ...

The MOTHER seems dazed for a second, then lifts her head in a brief nod.

> BONIFACIO
>
> Any luck?

> DOLORES
>
> Next door got some enamel bowls and a coat.

No reply.

> BONIFACIO
>
> Mum?

> MOTHER
>
> I worked all night. Washed everything. He helped me.
> (*She indicates BONIFACIO*). For the honour. Every
> bit of fluff from the chair. We burned the other one,
> to give them a fire. Something to sit by. His chair.
> (*Pause.*) They said the house was too clean. I must
> have used soap. They said if I could afford soap, if we
> could afford a fire, then we didn't need anything.

Silence.

Then DOLORES knocks over the coffin with a clatter as she leaps to her feet.

DOLORES

They want us dirty!

She subsides and sits on the floor against the wall, biting her nails.
The MOTHER sits hunched by the fire, as before.

DOLORES

Anyway, sod the church.

BONIFACIO

Don't! You'll be damned! (*He crosses himself quickly.*)

DOLORES

Well, some God! He's only got a few favourites, the
rest of us can go to hell. I could do better myself.
Anyway, who wants to go to heaven? Sounds more
endless than down here.

MOTHER

(*Low, after a pause.*) Well, I hope your father's in hell.
At least it's warm down there, and he's used to the
dark. No ... I hope he's roasting.

BONIFACIO

Don't say that!

MOTHER

I'm glad. See him come home, black as pitch, to garlic
and water soup. I'm glad he's dead. Better than
being crippled. At least he's spared your father's
humiliation. I'm glad of that. No ... no, I'm not!!

It comes out as a howl, frightening the YOUNG ONES. She covers
her face in her shawl. DOLORES glowers. BONIFACIO moves to
comfort his MOTHER.

BONIFACIO

Don't worry. I'll look after you. They're letting me
work with dynamite. I can crawl in easier being
small.

His MOTHER rises, and the chair falls back.

There is a loud crump of an explosion. BONIFACIO jerks his jacket
over his head and throws himself offstage. The MOTHER runs off
separately.

DOLORES sings: 'Don't Take My Children.'

DOLORES

No!
Don't take my children ...
Take my man if you must.
No, don't take my man.
How
How can I feed them?
I have no man.
I have no man.
My son,
Where are you going?
Into the dark,
Into the deep mines with dynamite!
No, no, no!
There was plenty of flesh to eat then.
No, no, no!

Light change.

ACT ONE – SCENE FOUR

At the end of the song, DOLORES crosses as a laid table is brought on. She changes her cap and apron, and lays the table.

A trumpeting WOMAN'S VOICE makes her jump.

SENORA LOPEZ

(Off.) And don't forget the soup spoons!

DOLORES tries and fails to fold a napkin, and is alerted by a loud 'Pssst' from the open window.

A black face looms as a YOUNG MINER jumps up and is gone. She leans out, and runs away from the window as a heavily built and tightly- corseted WOMAN enters with a vase of hideous flowers.

SENORA LOPEZ

Are you done? I don't want that joint spoiling!
(She thrusts the vase at DOLORES who receives it
reverently and puts it on the table.) Not there ... in
the middle! Tch, they've no idea, no idea at all.

She puts the flowers in the middle of the table, and checks the level of the decanter with a sharp look at DOLORES, and goes.

DOLORES runs to the window as the YOUNG MINER hops over the sill and grabs her.

DOLORES

You fool. She'll be back any minute!

MINER

Give us a kiss then.

DOLORES

You'll make me all dirty!

MINER

Do more than that to you. Made your mind up yet? I
shouldn't dwell ... others willing.

DOLORES

Oh, are they?

MINER

Come on, Dolores. Make up your mind. It's not fair to
keep a man waiting.

DOLORES

I know.

They embrace swiftly, with mutual passion. Then he takes a quick
gulp at the decanter as she dabs at the coal dust on her apron, then
pushes him out.

MINER

Right! (*Straddling the window sill.*) Those buggers on
the Navarre shift! Think they can top our output?
Not a chance!

He leaps off the sill. There is a crash and a yell.

DOLORES

(*Leaning out.*) Serves you right! (*She turns from the
window, tidying her hair and straightening her cap.*)
That's how they get more work out of you.

She adds water to the decanter. She tastes the wine, adds sugar,
then salt, tastes, and nods, satisfied.

The WOMAN enters, followed by a SMALL MAN who makes a
covert gesture to DOLORES, who ignores him. They drink their
soup, the MAN slurping to his WIFE'S annoyance.

DOLORES exits and returns at once with the joint, putting it on the
table by the window.

SENORA LOPEZ

(*Sipping delicately.*) Quite a good wine this time.

SENOR LOPEZ

(*Knocking it back.*) Should be, at the price. (*Nods to DOLORES, gooses her as she refills his glass.*) Never does to buy rubbish. (*Drains it again.*)

SENORA LOPEZ

(*Leans back to DOLORES.*) You'll be needed Sunday.

DOLORES

But I haven't had a day off since I been here!

SENOR LOPEZ

That's enough. Plenty of girls where you come from.

He looks up at her resentfully as she refills his glass. She gives him a look of sexual contempt and moves off.

SENORA LOPEZ

What are you doing?

DOLORES

I thought I heard a dog ... I was worried about the meat. (*She has no confidence in this excuse.*)

SENORA LOPEZ

And where, pray, is the water?

DOLORES brings the pitcher, plonks it on the table. The SENORA rises in a rage.

SENORA LOPEZ

How many more times! I will not, not, not drink from a pitcher like a common peasant!

SENOR LOPEZ

My love! (*As she knocks the pitcher over in her fury.*)

SENORA LOPEZ

Now look what you've done, she's broken it! She's
broken the pitcher! I saw what you were doing,
leaning out of the window, you vulgar, common slut!
They bring their filth in with them. It's no good,
Gonzalo, she'll have to go. What can you expect from
such a background?

DOLORES

That's it.

She throws down the knife and fork, and the napkin from her
shoulder and goes.

SENORA LOPEZ

Where's she gone? Come back when I speak to you!
She can't go unless I tell her to! Have you been up to
your tricks again?

SENOR LOPEZ

Me? No.

SENORA LOPEZ

(*Pinging the bell furiously.*) I will not put up with it.
Bad enough living in a filthy miners' town – horrible
black creatures with their horrible eyes looming at
you ...

She picks up the knife and fork, turns for the joint. DOLORES bobs
up, grabs the joint, and is gone.

SENORA LOPEZ

Everywhere you look, nothing but black filth! The
meat! Where's the meat? The meat's gone!

The sound of a 'dog' barking.

Light change.

ACT ONE – SCENE FIVE

The music of 'Marriage' to a pipe and drum.

SENOR and SENORA LOPEZ remove the table.

The WEDDING GUESTS enter in pairs to the music, bearing modest gifts, a towel, a cup, a brush, and two small stools on open hands. Nothing is new – nor are the clothes of the guests – but all are decked in wild flowers.

DOLORES and her HUSBAND enter last. They lead the dance and the song 'Marriage.'

> Marriage,
> The great solution,
> Marriage,
> To be wed.
> For all the girls of our village,
> The answer to life's mystery
> Is in bed.
> Marriage,
> The great solution,
> What good's marriage
> Without bread?
> Who feels like shagging
> On an empty stomach?
> When you're young you fight
> But when the child comes
> It says
> Feed me
> Feed me ...
> And the child has to be fed.

As the song and the ENSEMBLE dance ends, DOLORES and her HUSBAND dance alone.

ACT ONE

The MUSIC ends.

The OTHERS leave. DOLORES and her HUSBAND sit across from each other on the wedding stools. As she throws off her shawl, we see she is pregnant. She picks up a book and reads.

Her HUSBAND fidgets and sighs, almost a groan.

                    DOLORES
Get out then. Go for a walk!

                    HUSBAND
What for?

                    DOLORES
I don't know ... exercise!

                    HUSBAND
It'll only make me feel hungry.

DOLORES sees the sense of this, and looks at him unobserved in brief anguish. A pause. They both sigh.

                    DOLORES
Not much of a job. Only in summer. (*She hugs her shawl about her.*)

                    HUSBAND
You know it bloody floods ... every bloody winter!

                    DOLORES
Anyway, how can you be sure they'll have you back come spring?

                    HUSBAND
Oh, they'll have me. Till forty. Over forty, finish. Well, they slow you up, the old'uns.

DOLORES

What about when you're old? What are you going to do
then? Live on roast air?

HUSBAND

We're lucky. Down the valley, they're closing up.

DOLORES

It's true then?

HUSBAND

Yes. Confirmed. All three pits going.

DOLORES

(Mutters.) And what have you done about it?

HUSBAND

Me? (Laughs in irritation.) What can I do?

DOLORES

Stop it.

HUSBAND

Oh yes. And how? How'm I going to do that? Am I the
boss?

DOLORES

Go on strike.

HUSBAND

Look – oh, never mind. You can't talk to women.

DOLORES

(Quietly.) Why not?

HUSBAND

Look. They're closing the pits because they're not
making enough money. They have to make a profit!

He gestures with a sort of violent triumph.

DOLORES

For who? Who's they?

HUSBAND

What do you mean?

DOLORES

Who's they?

HUSBAND

The owners!

DOLORES

What about us?

HUSBAND

(*Patient.*) They're the bosses. All very well say strike.

DOLORES

Why not? Strike – that's what I say!

HUSBAND

And starve. (*Pause.*) Mind you ... mind you, there comes a point. I mean, when they're trying to cut your legs off, what have you got to lose?

DOLORES

Something wrong somewhere. Shutting off people's lives. Can't be right.

HUSBAND

You worry about us, gal.

She gives him a glare, picks up her book.

HUSBAND

Makes you think, though. I couldn't do that to people.

She turns a page. He belches.

DOLORES

Don't.

HUSBAND

I can't help it, it's wind.

DOLORES

What am I supposed to do, cook stones?

A pause. He rises.

DOLORES

Where are you going?

HUSBAND

Out.

He crosses, puts on his cap under her resentful eye, hovers, indecisive, and goes.

DOLORES

I'll be on me own!

He goes. DOLORES makes to follow him, not to be left on her own. But she falters, and changes her mind. She picks up a tattered book.

DOLORES sings: 'They Can't Stop You Reading.'

DOLORES

They can't stop you reading,

They can't stop you reading.

If you have eyes, that is,

Eyes able to see.

And if there are books,

Books . . .

Books with information.

Books with information.

They can't stop you reading.

No, they can't stop you reading,

They can't
Stop
You
Reading ...

Light change.

ACT ONE – SCENE SIX

Outside the mine.

THREE MEN on strike, including DOLORES' HUSBAND. THE MANAGER arrives with his briefcase.

MANAGER

Now lads, what's it all about?

HUSBAND

You know what it's about. More money.

MINER TWO

Our own co-op ...

MINER ONE

Buy food off you, we can't afford it.

HUSBAND

You pay us and take it back!

MINER TWO

I got four children to feed ...

MANAGER

Hang on, hang on, hang on! I'm the manager, not God.

MINER TWO

No need for blasphemy.

MANAGER

Now, be reasonable. Perfectly willing to listen.

HUSBAND

We've been to the Union.

MINER ONE

They're sending someone.

MINER TWO

You'll have to listen to him.

HUSBAND

Could end in a strike.

MANAGER

Don't you blackmail me, son.

MINER ONE

True though. It's what we pay the Union for.

MANAGER

I don't have to see him.

MEN

You do! You do! Oh, yes you do!

MANAGER

It's a free country. (*They laugh. The MANAGER goes inside, turns at the door.*) I'll tell you this, if I know anything about unions, he'll be a damn sight more reasonable than you lot. Now get out of my way.

He goes in.

The MEN are elated by the confrontation, but their euphoria deflates and they kick about, worried. DOLORES arrives with a CHILD on her hip. She is very pregnant. ANOTHER WOMAN accompanies her – EMILIA.

DOLORES

Is he here?

MINER TWO

Not yet.

MINER ONE

Should have been on the eight o'clock. Bugger never
showed up.

MINER TWO

He'll be here.

HUSBAND

Heard that before.

EMILIA

Oh you, your shift always talks tough.

DOLORES

If it wasn't for our meetings, you'd have been back,
tails between your legs!

MINER TWO

All we want's a fair do. We're not looking for trouble.

EMILIA

Looking for it? We're in it! I'm in trouble, she's in
trouble ... Christ, who isn't in trouble? (*Laughter.*)

The UNION MAN arrives, with a little cardboard case.

UNION

You seem pretty cheerful. Luis Barreno.

He shakes hands with the MEN.

HUSBAND

My wife, Dolores.

UNION

Oh. Yes. *(He gives her a sharp look, he has heard of her. DOLORES returns his look with a steady stare. He turns to the MEN.)* Well now, lads, let's have it.

MINER ONE

What's it going to be? Them or us?

UNION

Ooh, steady on, mister … not that simple.

DOLORES

It's simple enough. We're starving.

The others murmur assent.

UNION

I know, I know lads. That's why I'm here. Oh, a couple of points before I go in. I've read your complaints, now there's no way they're going to grant all this. *(DOLORES laughs. Heflicks her a glance.)* I know you know that …

HUSBAND

No, we don't.

UNION

Well, let me tell you how it's done. How we go about it …

DOLORES

'We'!

UNION

Your wife, is she?

HUSBAND

(Unsmiling.) Yes.

UNION

Fine woman.

MINER ONE

A bit mouthy!

UNION

You said it, brother, not me. *(He draws the MEN away from the TWO WOMEN.)* Now. It's like this. You ask for more than you know you got a chance of. They offer as little as they think they can get away with ... Tara! You meet in the middle.

MINER TWO

What we're asking for is bare survival.

UNION

I know. I know. But we got to be practical. Rome wasn't built in a day.

EMILIA

(Mystified.) What's Rome go to do with it?

HUSBAND

We only want what's fair.

MINER ONE

What's right.

MINER TWO

All we're asking's enough to keep ourselves alive ... it's common justice.

UNION

Oh dear, oh oh oh! *(He laughs.)* If we could have that for the asking, I'd be out of a job for a start! Oh dear! Look ... lads ... justice and the law – well, not the same thing, is it? We got the law, make no mistake

about that ... What's more, my job's to see we stay
well within it or we're in trouble. Now, we don't want
trouble. Any set-to, that just gives them ammunition.
There you are you see? Nothing but a herd of clowns
and ruffians who don't know how it works. That
would suit the bosses – see us make fools of ourselves.
All they have to do then is shout troublemakers –
stick the lot of you inside!

DOLORES

The voice of sweet reason.

UNION

(*To DOLORES.*) Now look here, young woman, you
listen to me. I haven't come all this way to be cheeked
by a bloody female. I don't care whose wife you are.
I'm here on official union business and I've come a
fair distance on your behalf ...

DOLORES

Walked, did you?

UNION

I came by train.

DOLORES

Who paid your fare? I've never been on a train. (*To
EMILIA.*) You been on a train? (*EMILIA shakes her
head.*) We paid your fare, mister. With empty bellies.

UNION

I've heard about you.

HUSBAND

(*To DOLORES.*) Shut up.

MINER TWO

That's enough, gal. *(To UNION MAN.)* How are we
doing? We got a good case, but we're feeling it.

UNION

I know. And I'm here to negotiate. That's what I'm
here for. No point in obstruction. You've got the bull by
the tail. If you're not reasonable, you can't expect the
bosses to be reasonable when they've got the bull by the
tail.

DOLORES

Cowshit.

UNION

Will somebody get this bloody woman out of it!

Her HUSBAND casually turns, gives her a cuff over the head,
sending her reeling. The OTHERS move apart, in earnest
conversation with the UNION MAN. DOLORES hold her aching head.

The conversation reaches agreement. The MEN nod. DOLORES
draws close to listen. The UNION MAN, with a wave of his hand,
goes inside.

They wait.

DOLORES scowls at her HUSBAND. He flexes his shoulders. He has
to be seen to act like a man. The OTHER MEN avoid her eyes.

The MEN pace, waiting. MINER ONE, feeling optimistic, lifts a
thumb as he passes MINER TWO, the older man. He waves in reply.
The UNION MAN appears briefly, and speaks to them. They seem
undecided, but he reassures them and disappears inside again.

MINER ONE

I think he's going to do it for us.

MINER TWO

Yes, he's a good man.

MINER ONE

One of us.

MUSIC underneath.

DOLORES and EMILIA whisper together and laugh. This makes the MEN uneasy.

The MUSIC stops.

The MANAGER comes out with the UNION MAN. They talk to the MEN, excluding the WOMEN. There are sober nods. The MEN pick up their gear. But they are depressed.

MINER ONE

Come on, they'll be docking us.

EMILIA bursts into tears.

HUSBAND

(To DOLORES.) Referred to arbitration.

DOLORES

(To the UNION MAN as he shakes hands briskly all round, preparing to leave.) Didn't take you long to sell us out.

UNION

That's libel – that's slander, that is.

MANAGER

Move away from the gate.

DOLORES

Take your hands off me.

HUSBAND

Leave her alone.

MANAGER

Come on! Inside, or clear this gate! (*A scuffle. The
MANAGER shouts:*) Police!

Enter THREE POLCEMEN.

DOLORES' HUSBAND is manhandled off. The MEN go, fighting to
resist arrest.

Light change.

ACT ONE – SCENE SEVEN

Dolores' House.

The sound of a CHILD crying, off. DOLORES, white-faced, sits by
a crib. A knock. She turns her head absently. Another knock, and
then a well-dressed YOUNG WOMAN enters tentatively.

THE DONA

Dolores?

DOLORES looks up and across at her.

DOLORES

(*Inclines her head slightly.*) Dona Sebastiana.

DONA

Oh please, just my name. We're old friends!

DOLORES

(*Low.*) What do you want? (*The DONA gestures
uncertainly, remaining near the door.*) You heard
that I had triplets? News travels.

DONA

I...

DOLORES

If you've come to see the sights you're too late. There's only one left, and she won't last long. (*She glances briefly at the crib.*)

DONA

Oh! How very sad! Tch! And your husband not with you. May I ... ? (*Despite herself, she can't resist crossing for a peep into the cot.*) Oh!! Ohh, she's like a little doll! A tiny, tiny doll! (*She wants to pick the BABY up but restrains herself.*) Oh Dolores! Oh!! And you lost your first little girl. How old was she?

DOLORES

Three.

DONA

And the baby last year ... tch ... but your little boy ... Reuben, isn't it? He's well? (*Raising her voice above the CHILD'S fretful cry, off.*)

The sound frets away to silence.

DOLORES

(*Hoarse.*) Sit down.

The DONA looks about, dusts off the stool discreetly, and sits.

DONA

And your husband? Still ... ?

DOLORES

In prison. Yes.

DONA

Oh Dolores. How dreadful. (*She looks round the empty room.*) And nothing coming in? (*DOLORES looks at her but does not reply.*) I see you still have

your sewing machine. That must bring you in a few
pennies. I could give you some work myself if you
could make me a price.

DOLORES

I'm too weak to work.

DONA

Oh. We-ell, if you like ... *(She gives the sewing
machine a quick once-over.)* I'll buy your machine
from you. My maid could use it for the children's
dresses. I'd give you a good price for it. Only if you
want to, of course.

DOLORES, unable to speak, lowers her head.

DONA

You mustn't give way. Blessed are those who suffer in
the Name of the Lord. It is the Lord's privilege,
Dolores.

DOLORES

(Looks up.) I'm privileged?

DONA

Think of the reward in heaven.

A pause. DONA SEBASTIANA leans forward and puts her hand, in
its lavender glove, on DOLORES' knee.

DONA

Dolores ... Dolores I can help you. Please! For old
times' sake! At school, you were the brightest. You
were cleverer than any of us. It's awful to see you like
this.

DOLORES makes no response.

DONA

I . . . I've been talking to some of my friends. It might
be possible . . . We were thinking that we would like to
find you a little house, with a piece of land and some
cattle, a few fowls to get you started. And a job for
your husband when he . . . when he . . .

Despite herself, DOLORES looks up.

DOLORES

(*Her voice hoarse.*) Why me? You can't help us all.
Why me?

DONA

As a friend.

She rises and crosses and looks into the cot again.

DONA

Have you named her?

DOLORES

Amaya. (*Clears her throat.*) Amaya.

DONA

(*Murmurs into the crib.*) Amaya? Oh, I want to pick
her up.

DOLORES gestures permission for her to do so.

DOLORES

What difference does it make, she won't last.

DONA

Could I? (*She picks up the BABY.*) Just like a little doll
in a crèche at Christmas – a little Christ child! (*She
approaches DOLORES, the BABY in her arms.*)
Think about it.

She walks about, rocking the CHILD. Then she puts the CHILD down gently, cooing to it and putting the cover over gently. She rises, crosses to DOLORES, and kneels at her side. Again, she puts her hand on DOLORES' knee. DOLORES seems mesmerised by the sight of the pale glove.

DONA

It could all be yours.

DOLORES

You'd give me a house?

DONA

Yes!

DOLORES

With land?

DONA

A few acres, enough. And animals, and a well. Think of it, dear Dolores, clean water for the children! You want them to grow up fit and strong, your little boy and this poor little thing. She's going to need a lot of care! (DOLORES looks up at her in naked agony.) Now if you were to put all your attention, all your care, into your dear babies – after all, it's what we were created for. Women have a very special responsibility. If we neglect our children ...

DOLORES

You think I neglect my children? You think my children die from neglect?

DONA

No of course not ...

DOLORES

I haven't eaten bread for two weeks. How can I
make milk for one baby, let alone three, on mouldy
potatoes?

DONA

I'm sorry. I didn't mean to upset you.

DOLORES

You smell of butter.

DONA

I want to help you!

DOLORES

Do you? And the conditions?

DONA

I'm sorry?

DOLORES

Oh come! Of course, there are conditions. Your lot
would never give something for nothing.

DONA

(*Slight pause.*) Well, naturally we'd expect you to –
build up the place ... you and your husband. There
would be plenty to keep you occupied.

DOLORES

I see. You want to bribe us to be quiet.

DONA

I'm simply asking you to put your children first.

DOLORES

(*With difficulty.*) That is what I am doing. I am trying
to do just that.

DONA

(Pause.) Believe me, all I want is to help you. As a
friend. It's nothing to do with politics, as far as I'm
concerned.

DOLORES

(Slight pause.) They've made a lackey of you.

Pause. Then the DONA dives into her purse. She is embarrassed to
be dealing directly with money.

DONA

Please. *(There is no response.)* At least let me give . . .
*(She proffers the money. DOLORES flicks the merest
glance and looks in her lap. SEBASTIANA, deeply
embarrassed and not knowing what to do, eventually
lays the money at DOLORES' feet. She rises.)* I'll send
you some more, as soon as I can. I promise! Come to
the house. Come and see me, I can give you clothes . . .
baby things. Please, say you'll come! (But there is
no response from DOLORES. The DONA prepares to
leave.)* I'll pray for you.

Still no response. On an impulse, she opens her purse and empties
it on the table and goes, with an in-drawn sob, and a handkerchief
to her eyes.

DOLORES pauses for a second, then picks up the money at her feet,
moves to the table and counts the money with concentration.

The CHILD makes a sound. She puts the money down, crosses to
the crib, and picks up the CHILD.

She sings the lullaby 'Sweet Water.'

DOLORES

Sweet water in the well,
Cow's breath is sweet.

Sweet milk,

Sweet hay,

So sweet.

No choice.

No choice.

Bread on the table,

Fire in the hearth.

Sweet apple,

Sweet linen,

Too sweet.

No choice.

No choice.

At the end, she peers at the BABY, studying its face.

DOLORES

Still here then?

Light change.

ACT ONE – SCENE EIGHT

THE GOVERNOR of the prison at his desk. Women's voices. He rings his bell, his SECRETARY appears.

GOVERNOR

What's going on?

SECRETARY

It's the women, sir.

GOVERNOR

Women?

SECRETARY

With grievances.

GOVERNOR

Grievances? What grievances?

SECRETARY

They feel that their husbands . . .

GOVERNOR

(*Making her jump.*) Don›t waste my time with tattle!
Tell them to submit through the proper channels.

SECRETARY

Yes, we have advised them on procedure, but it is a
question of the children. It is the children, you see.

GOVERNOR

Get rid of them.

He waves her off, returns to his papers. But she does not go. He
looks up.

SECRETARY

They won't go sir.

GOVERNOR

Won't go. What do you mean, won't go?

SECRETARY

(*Very humbly.*) They're lying on the tram tracks, sir.

GOVERNOR

What for?

SECRETARY

(*Softly.*) As a protest, sir.

GOVERNOR

Rubbish. Move them.

SECRETARY

They've selected a delegation.

GOVERNOR

Oh, have they?

SECRETARY

Hoping for the honour of . . .

GOVERNOR

No.

SECRETARY

(*Softly.*) It wouldn't take a minute, sir.

GOVERNOR

(*Making her jump.*) I'm not having them in here.
Tell them . . .

EMILIA, DOLORES, and JUANITA enter.

GOVERNOR

Get out! What are you doing in here?

EMILIA

We're here to see you.

He gets up, walks the line, inspecting each of them.

JUANITA

We've . . . come a long way.

He gazes at DOLORES, who gazes back.

GOVERNOR

Is one of you the one they call Pasionaria?

The WOMEN exchange a brief, self-conscious smile.

EMILIA

We've come because our husbands are being held
without trial.

JUANITA

And they haven't done anything!

EMILIA

So, we're asking you ...

JUANITA

... for your help ...

EMILIA

... to release them.

He walks the line again, glaring into their faces.

GOVERNOR

Improperly submitted petitions can be neither received nor considered.

DOLORES

(*Low.*) We have petitioned.

GOVERNOR

(*Not hearing her well.*) What?

EMILIA

(*Quick.*) You didn't reply.

JUANITA

We never got an answer.

GOVERNOR

Precisely. You have your answer. There's nothing for you here. I'm not prepared to deal with this.

SECRETARY

But sir ...

EMILIA

You're not prepared to deal with us?

JUANITA

There's a lot of women out there! (*The GOVERNOR looks out the window.*)

GOVERNOR

Your husbands were arrested at illegal meetings where subversive literature was being dispersed. They are being held by Security Headquarters.

JUANITA

The order came from you. You signed it.

EMILIA

You put them in – you get them out!

GOVERNOR

You won't be helped by insolence!

JUANITA

Those children out there are hungry!

GOVERNOR

And whose fault is that? You're subversives, the lot of you!

JUANITA

I'm not! I don't know what it means.

GOVERNOR

Clear off to Russia if you think it's so marvellous!

EMILIA

What's he on about? What's Russia got to do with it?

JUANITA

Yeah, keep to the point.

ACT ONE

GOVERNOR

(*Banging desk, making them all jump.*) I repeat! I can
do nothing. I will transmit your requests, if and when
properly submitted, via the correct channels to the
proper authorities. Beyond that I am not empowered.

Pause. DOLORES clears her throat.

DOLORES

(*Quietly.*) I suggest that you take action now.

GOVERNOR

And why, pray, should I do that?

DOLORES

Because ... if you don't ... we shall stay ... outside
your window ... day and night ... with our children.

GOVERNOR

Oh, you will, will you? We'll see about ...

DOLORES

To be followed by others if you arrest us. And others,
because there are plenty of us. And we'll shout our
petition to the city until the walls fall about your fat
ears. Until you take your fat head out of your fat arse
and start using it to think! (*Making him jump, and
the SECRETARY to giggle, covering her mouth.*) To
think about who you are. What you're doing. To your
neighbours. To your countrymen. To your friends. Till
you see just what it is that you, the child of your mother,
the son of your father, a man – a human being – just what
you – not Security, not the judges, not the government,
not the military, but what you – a man born within
the walls of this city – what you are doing to your own
people, your neighbours ... What you are doing to the

innocent, the falsely accused, the improperly detained –
to all those people whose lives you are destroying by
blackmail, by oppression, by imprisonment and by
torture. And if you believe that what you do is invisible
to the citizens of this province, then let me tell you
that every Spaniard from here to Granada knows your
name. Every man, every woman, every child. Each and
every one capable of revenge. At any time. Day or night.
Twenty-four hours a day. Remember that when you
pick up your hat for a stroll. Consider carefully as you
cross the square to go to Mass. Be reminded as you step
outside, hoping to reach home safely after an 'honest'
day's work. Meanwhile, we'll sit outside your walls.

They go.

> GOVERNOR

Quick, get me an outside line!

But the SECRETARY'S eyes are shining, her mouth open.

> GOVERNOR

Move!

The SECRETARY jumps, and leaps for the telephone.

Light change.

ACT ONE – SCENE EIGHT

A prison cell with bunk-beds.

DOLORES enters, followed by a NUN.

> NUN

Take off your clothes please.

ACT ONE

DOLORES

I've already been searched.

NUN

I have to examine you for disease. Please take your
clothes off. There's no need to be embarrassed.

DOLORES

I'm sorry, no.

NUN

Take your clothes off.

DOLORES

I'm sorry, no.

The NUN goes. The THREE OTHER WOMEN in the cell cheer.

DOLORES

Where do I sleep?

LUISA

Up there. (*They wait, ready to jeer. She leaps up like
a cat.*)

PILAR

(*Laughs.*) We know your game! (*DOLORES looks down
in enquiry.*) I'm one meself. Dipper.

DOLORES looks round, puzzled.

LUISA

Pickpocket? Nah, not 'er. She's a civilian.

MANUELA

What's she doing here?

PILAR

(*To DOLORES, nodding towards MANUELA.*) Be
careful.

NUN

Lights out!

The lights are lowered. PILAR mutters prayers.

LUISA

Pack it in.

PILAR

(Getting off her knees, mild.) Well, you never know.
Be on the safe side. Christ, I'm hungry.

Pause.

LUISA

Had a guy last week, all I had to do was comb his hair
while he read the paper. Paid me full whack.

MANUELA

Shut up, you fucker, I'm trying to sleep.

DOLORES

You're not the only one!

Silence.

LUISA

(Whispers to DOLORES.) That wasn't very clever.

PILAR

(Whispers.) Slit a nun's gizzard open last year.
(Aloud.) She didn't mean it, Manuela.

Fade to low light, then to black.

Slow fade up to daylight.

An ELECTRIC BELL – loud and piercing. The WOMEN tumble out,
cursing, and dress. DOLORES stays in her bunk.

PILAR

Hey, get up!

DOLORES

What for?

PILAR

They'll be after you!

DOLORES

They've already got me.

MANUELA laughs, surprising the OTHERS.

MANUELA

What are you in for?

DOLORES

Politics.

MANUELA

(Uninterested.) Oh.

LUISA

Politics?

DOLORES

(Shrugs.) I like to eat.

LUISA

Yeah but, you're a woman.

DOLORES

A woman runs this place.

MANUELA

That fucking bitch.

DOLORES

(Sudden rage.) Half the world's fucking women!

PILAR

Yeah, and the other half's men.

DOLORES

Who makes them? (*Still in a rage.*)

PILAR

We do.

LUISA

Yeah, then they bash our heads in.

PILAR

Like my old man says: if you want to keep your teeth, don't argue.

LUISA

What you trying to do? What you after?

DOLORES looks at her sourly.

PILAR

Money!

MANUELA laughs.

LUISA

(*Rolling up her bedding.*) Nah, it's a joke. Fucking stupid.

DOLORES punches her.

LUISA

Aoww! What you do that for?

DOLORES

Fucking smile off your face, that's all.

Silence.

LUISA

(*Holding her jaw.*) Oh, I see. That's politics. Fucking
hitting people.

DOLORES, depressed at her own rage, sits, her head in her hands.

LUISA

Thanks very much. I'll remember that when you want
me vote. If I had one.

A tense silence. MANUELA crosses to DOLORES.

MANUELA

Where's your cup?

DOLORES looks up.

DOLORES

Haven't got one.

MANUELA

(*Grabs PILAR'S cup, gives it to DOLORES.*) You have
now.

PILAR

Hey!

The NUN enters, stands by the exit. The WOMEN cross to
workbenches, and pick up their sewing. DOLORES remains, her
arms folded.

NUN

(*Crosses to DOLORES.*) If you continue to refuse to
work, you'll be sent to the punishment cells.

She goes out. The WOMEN whisper. The NUN returns with the
WOMAN GOVERNOR.

GOVERNOR

Stand up.

DOLORES remains seated.

After a pause.

GOVERNOR

Why are you refusing to work?

DOLORES

Because I'm not being paid, because none of us is being paid. *(To the OTHERS:)* Stop working!

Tentatively, they stop working.

DOLORES

Don't work! They can't send us all to the punishment cells.

PILAR puts down her needle decisively. The GOVERNOR whispers to the NUN who exits quickly. The WOMEN sit, the GOVERNOR waits, the NUN returns, whispers in her ear.

GOVERNOR

You will return to your cells. *(The WOMEN rise, DOLORES makes to follow.)* Not you. Wait.

The OTHERS leave.

GOVERNOR

I'm transferring you to a single cell.

DOLORES

Why?

GOVERNOR

And I'll see that you get books.

DOLORES

Books?

GOVERNOR

As a political prisoner, you're entitled to that.

DOLORES

Special treatment?

GOVERNOR

(*Showing her a newspaper.*) As you see, you're
becoming quite famous. We must look after you.

DOLORES looks at her picture with interest.

GOVERNOR

It doesn't do you justice. (*DOLORES flicks her a look.*)

DOLORES

I don't want to be moved.

GOVERNOR

In here, what you want is of no importance.

DOLORES

All right. If you're prepared for the consequences.
They'll know it's because you're afraid of my
influence.

GOVERNOR

I see. Blackmail.

DOLORES

I want to stay in my cell, and I want to hold meetings.

GOVERNOR

Hah!

DOLORES

The conditions here are now so appalling you've got
a near riot on your hands. You're understaffed, and
local politics are in such a mess you'll be lucky to pay
the wages by the end of the month.

GOVERNOR

Oh, you politicals! You know it all, don't you? You
strut about, thinking you're a cut above ...

DOLORES

(Tired.) No. We're as idle and backsliding as
everybody else. But at least we have a point.

GOVERNOR

What point? To be a social nuisance?

DOLORES

If that's the point, yes. What's yours? What's your
point?

GOVERNOR

To bear enormous responsibility and carry out
orders.

DOLORES

Oh orders, yes, you do that very well, you're very
obedient – well, it takes away the strain, doesn't it?
No decisions necessary, just do as they say and go to
church on Sundays. Good God woman, you're one of
us! What do you do for us? Do you think you've got a
mind ... a soul, to use as a click-beetle for six days of
the week?

The WOMEN stare at each other.

GOVERNOR

You have no idea.

DOLORES

Yes, I do. I know exactly what could be done for these
women.

The GOVERNOR looks at her, turns and goes.

DOLORES sings: 'They Can't Stop You Reading.'

DOLORES

They can't stop you reading,

They can't stop you reading.

If you have eyes, that is,

Eyes able to see.

And if there are books,

Books ...

Books with information.

Books with information.

My eyes are my mind,

I see with my mind,

And my mind reads books,

Books,

Books which inform me.

I am in receipt of information.

They can't stop you reading,

They can't stop you reading.

No, they can't stop you reading,

They can't

Stop

You

Reading ...

ACT ONE – SCENE TEN

DOLORES and MANUELA.

MANUELA

What are you miserable about, I've got twelve years.
(*DOLORES does not reply.*) Your kids? Was that your

boy outside the window last night?

DOLORES

Don't laugh, he wanted to come in. He's got nowhere to sleep. *(She sighs heavily.)* Not a word from anybody. I might as well be dead.

MANUELA

Forgotten about you, have they?

DOLORES

There's been trouble. A split.

MANUELA

(Laughs.) Oh. They've fallen out.

DOLORES

Poor old party hacks, stuck it for years, now they're all being kicked downstairs.

MANUELA

What for?

DOLORES

(Bleak.) Because they're holding us back. *(MANUELA is surprised at her tone.)* They don't speak for Spain any more.

MANUELA

And you reckon you do? Come off it – who cares about Spain? Look out for yourself, mate. No other bugger will. Anyway, you're on the wrong side.

DOLORES

Oh?

MANUELA

You wanna get in with the businessmen, the lackeys ... that's how you get on. All your lot does is get chucked inside and called traitors.

DOLORES

Do you think that's what I am? A traitor?

MANUELA

Yeah, course you are! You're a troublemaker. Trying
to upset everything, bring down the government,
whatever you're trying to do. I might be a criminal,
but I love the royal family. I'm loyal, mate.

DOLORES

(*Looking out of the window.*) When I was at a rally in
Toledo, I saw a boy pick a dead lettuce leaf out of a pile
of dung and eat it.

MANUELA

People are fools, idiots.

DOLORES

You mean we should all thieve, like you?

MANUELA

Yeah. Like them.

DOLORES throws back her head, laughing.

MANUELA

Listen, people only dole out when it suits them, or to
save their conscience.

DOLORES

(*Laughs.*) Conscience!?

MANUELA

Oh, I know you think I ain't got one – listen, the
reason I cut up that nun is because she was vicious.
(*Grins, wolfish.*) Same as me. Anyway … people think
being a criminal's being bad – like a rotten orange.

It's all rubbish. You got good and bad in you, same as
everybody else. It's just the way things happen. The
way your life turns out. Could be you, anybody.

DOLORES

Yeah.

MANUELA

It's not a bad life, thieving – well, bar this side of it.
You couldn't say it was reliable. The people you meet
aren't what you call dependable. (*Sighing piously.*)
Still, least it ain't boring.

DOLORES

Sounds like politics. Except, of course, that politics is
boring. (*She gazes out of the window.*)

MANUELA

How long do you reckon you're in for?

DOLORES

(*Turns, savage.*) Bastards won't bring me to trial ...
five or six years, I know it!

A bomb. They throw themselves flat.

Rising ride of sound, hooters, rifle-shots, cheers. A BAND plays.
They pick themselves up, dazed, and dust off their clothes.

The GOVERNOR enters.

GOVERNOR

The crown has fallen.

MANUELA

What?!

DOLORES

The government?

GOVERNOR

Resigned. Spain is a Republic.

She and DOLORES stare at each other.

DOLORES

Are they dead?

GOVERNOR

The Royal Family? *(She shakes her head.)* They've
left the country. *(DOLORES continues to stare at her.)*
I've received orders that all political prisoners are to
be released.

The NUN enters with DOLORES' coat and a small brown paper
parcel of her belongings.

GOVERNOR

You're free.

MANUELA turns away to the wall.

DOLORES takes the coat and the parcel, gives them to MANUELA
who takes them with aggressive quickness.

GOVERNOR

You'll need your coat.

DOLORES

I'm free.

She exchanges a quick nod with MANUELA, and turns to go.

The GOVERNOR, by the exit, holds out a hand in order to shake
hands. DOLORES pauses, but does not take it.

DOLORES

We're on opposite sides.

She goes quickly.

Fade to black

ACT TWO

<u>ACT TWO – SCENE ONE</u>

Upstage the KING and QUEEN leave by train.

EMILIA

So, Spain … became a Republic! The King and Queen
left – the cheers and thanks of devoted Spaniards
ringing in their ears.

Boos from the CROWD. A few things are thrown.

EMILIA

A new day, as they say, dawned!

The PEDLAR enters downstage, watches for a moment, and goes.

The CROWD circles and becomes a procession, carrying poles with
streamers.

MUSIC and DANCE. A PERFORMING BEAR.

CARLOS and JOSEFINA do a solo, watched by her MOTHER, who
pulls the GIRL away at the end of the dance.

CARLOS

Josefina!

The CROWD laugh as the MOTHER marches off with the GIRL. A
hand-bell is rung. A HEAVILY-BUILT MAN, LUIS, stands on a cart,
lifts his hand for silence.

LUIS

Friends! *(Laughs as they cheer.)* A bit of bad news.
As you know, we were hoping to have somebody
from the Central Committee to speak to us today.

Unfortunately, Pancho Sanchez, whom you all know well (*Cheers*) ... who was to have – I was going to say crown our day, but perhaps ... (*Cheers, whistles and laughter.*) Anyway, his train's stuck somewhere – (*Disagreement.*) I know, I know ... there you are ...

CROWD

Speech! Speech! Give us a speech! What about a speech, Luis?

LUIS

Me? No, no, not me. I'm no good on my feet.

He turns to the YOUNG MAN at his side.

LUIS

José?

JOSÉ

Too drunk.

LUIS turns to the QUIET MAN on his other side who shakes his head, smiling.

MANUEL

Not me, mate. (*He blows out his cheeks in alarm, causing laughter.*)

EMILIA

(*Calls out.*) What about Dolores?

LUIS

What about her?

EMILIA

Get Dolores to speak.

JOSEFINA

Yes Dolores!

She gets a cuff from her MOTHER, and is crushed by this and her own daring. CARLOS creeps up behind her and they begin to flirt circumspectly.

EMILIA

Come on Dolores ... Dolores!

DOLORES is standing with her HUSBAND and CHILDREN. She puts down her glass of beer and takes her CHILDREN by the hand, coming forward as much to show off her CHILDREN in their clean clothes as anything else.

DOLORES

What is it? What do you want?

The THREE MEN are undecided.

VOICE

Go on! Give 'er a chance!

Laughter and cheers. PEOPLE are drunk and happy.

LUIS

Well, if you like. Come on, Dolores. (*He shrugs
amiably to the MEN.*) Come on, no need to be shy. (*He
helps her up.*) As many of you know,
Dolores is one of the women just released from ...

Loud cheers. He waves a hand for silence.

LUIS

I'm sorry we haven't got a man to make the speech for
us, however ... (*Turns to DOLORES.*) I'm sure you'll
do your best. Don't worry. Take your time, gal. We're
all on your side.

DOLORES gives him an impenetrable look and steps forward.

DOLORES

(*After a pause.*) Thank you to those who helped us to come here, and who've given us hospitality. Sorry I lost the kids last night. Thank you again to those who helped me find them. I'll try not to let that happen again.

Laughter.

DOLORES

When I was in prison ... when I was in prison, I was called a traitor. I was called a traitor because I was a political. (*Shouts of disagreement.*) If to want to change things is to be a traitor, then we are all traitors. If to want to give the best of yourself is to be a traitor, then we're all traitors. If to want the best for the people of Spain is to be a traitor ...

She is drowned in shouts.

DOLORES

No. We're not traitors. But, I mean, who do we think we are? Saying we can change things? The working class? How can we be expected to organise a better life for anybody? Are we educated? Do we have power? Influence? No. They have it. The rich. The privileged. The army. The Church. The aristocrats. They have the power. They have the influence. And where has it got them?

VOICE

On our backs!

DOLORES

Right, brother! They want us to do as they say, obey their rules. Why? For whose advantage? Ours? Most people? The majority?

She laughs. Cheers and jeers.

> DOLORES

But then, what do we matter? Who are we? We're only the ignorant, the dirty, the lazy, idle good-for-nothings who deserve to stay where we belong ... *(Noise)* ... that's what we are ... *(Noise)* That's what they call us. The masses! The expendable majority. Friends, we are the majority! There are more of us. What can't we achieve? If we insist.

Cheers and shouts. She waits for silence.

> DOLORES

We have been denied our natural birthrights. Disinherited. What are these birthrights? I speak as a woman. I say they are the right to clean air to breathe, clean water to drink, a fair share of the means of existence, and the right to a den, a home, the same as any other animal. The rest is social contract. But air, water, food and shelter ... these are the bedrock of humanity ... of life itself – give or take the mosquito. *(She swats herself irritably.)* Look around you. Does your society, today, provide these basic rights? A fox, a wolf, a rabbit, even a rat has a better chance of rearing her litter to maturity than the majority ... the majority, friends, of the people of this country. I bore six children. How many do you see standing there? As for the notion of a life that could contain pleasure – culture – totally beyond our comprehension. We are the lower category. Beyond consideration. And we are the majority. Shall we be patient?

Shouts of 'No!'

DOLORES

Let those who now represent us fulfil their promises
to change ... change the face of this country. Feed,
educate and satisfy the needs of the people, the people
who are Spain ... Change everything. And if they
can't – we will.

Shouts and cheers. She waits for silence.

DOLORES

History ... is like a sleeping dragon. For hundreds
of years it lies in the cave. Suddenly, the animal is
awake. The dragon of Spain, friends, is awake. And
wagging its tail. (Quietly.) Who has the courage to
climb on its back?

Loud cheers. She is helped down and surrounded and congratulated.

LUIS, MANUEL and the YOUNG MAN draw aside to confer together.

LUIS

Ye-es, well.

JOSÉ

What do you think?

MANUEL

We could put her name forward. This area's still a
couple short on the central committee.

LUIS

No, can't have a woman.

MANUEL

I know what you mean. Pity. When it comes to
stepping forward ... Well, risky, isn't it, giving your
name ...

But they watch as, to their surprise, DOLORES takes names of supporters. LUIS crosses to have a word with her.

EMILIA takes over the list. DOLORES listens soberly to LUIS, picking up her DAUGHTER who runs to her.

The lights become mellow. MUSIC.

The COMPANY sing a Spanish song quietly, to round off the day.

CARLOS and JOSEFINA dance.

DOLORES listens to LUIS, the YOUNG MAN, JOSÉ, and MANUEL.

Twice her HUSBAND approaches. She reassures him that she won't be long.

End of song.

> *Lights to black.*

ACT TWO – SCENE TWO

A pavement cafe in Madrid.

Sitting are LUIS, MANUEL and JESUS, older. JESUS makes to refill MANUEL'S glass with brandy.

> MANUEL
>
> (*Modestly.*) Oh no, no ...

> LUIS
>
> Come on, you deserve it! We're proud of you both!

> MANUEL
>
> Thank you. (*He accepts more brandy.*) Your health.
>
> Oh, you should have heard her ...

They drink to Dolores, saying her name.

LUIS

Paris eh? What's it like – Madrid?

MANUEL

Yes and no.

LUIS

I wouldn't mind seeing Paris. Mind you, not the way
you did it.

JESUS

Pretty hard, was it?

MANUEL

A bit of a climb. *(They all laugh.)*

LUIS

Worth it, though. We're getting support. If the
Republic doesn't hold, God help the rest of Europe, the
way things stand ... well, that's my opinion.

EMILIA and DOLORES enter, in new clothes.

LUIS

Well, well, well!

DOLORES turns to display her new clothes.

EMILIA

I had to get a new dress to keep up with the Parisian
here.

LUIS

Very nice.

EMILIA

Is that an offer? *(Laughter.)*

JESUS

Well done, Dolores.

DOLORES

I'm afraid I did a bit of shopping. (*She gives LUIS and JESUS a small package each.*)

They open the presents ... silk ties.

JESUS

My word!

LUIS

Thanks! I'll do all right now.

DOLORES

I took a morning off.

JESUS

You deserve it. (*Kisses her in thanks.*)

LUIS

After crossing the bloody Pyrenees eh ... ?

EMILIA

Twice!

DOLORES

Never be the same again, eh Manuel? (*She starts to giggle.*)

MANUEL

Yes. What is it?

DOLORES

The ... the ... suit! (*She collapses in laughter.*)

MANUEL

(*Smiles.*) Oh. That.

EMILIA

What?

DOLORES

(To MANUEL:) You don't mind me ... ? *(He shakes his head shyly.)* Well, these Catalans, they're well named. They're like cats in the dark, only of course, we weren't used to the distances and climbing. We couldn't even whisper in case the frontier guards heard us. Anyway, we'd been going half the night when they got us in this cave – told us we had to cross a river. Remember the noise, Manuel?

MANUEL

Oh, we could hear it all right.

DOLORES

It sounded like Niagara Falls. Pitch dark, and we had to jump across these rocks, which we couldn't see. I mean, one false jump, you was drownded, I completely lost my nerve! Anyway, they got me across somehow between them. We're scrambling up the bank again when, all of a sudden, there's this mighty big splash behind me and the guide hisses and I think, he's gone, Manuel – oh, his poor wife and kids – it was thirty foot deep, and I'm thinking, we've lost him, he's gone, when all of a sudden, we hear this sort of low moaning ... "Me suit ... oh, me suit ... "

They all burst out laughing.

DOLORES

You see his own suit – you don't mind me telling – his own suit was in the pawn shop, so we got a tailor to run one up on instalments so's we'd look all right in Paris against all the intellectuals. So, poor old Manuel, never mind drowning, all he thinks about ...

EMILIA

Is the suit! *(Laughter.)*

MANUEL

Never mind. We got there.

DOLORES

Yes. At least they saw some real live Spaniards.
We were able to tell them the truth about what's
happening. You'd never believe the rubbish in the
international press. It's daft. We're fashionable. All
the students and intellectuals followed us around.
I wish it meant anything.

LUIS pours her a drink.

LUIS

A toast.

But they turn as there is a noise, offstage. The sound of shouting,
and car horns blaring.

DOLORES

(Shouting above the noise.) What is it?

MANUEL

Fascist demonstration in the square!

DOLORES

Do you think we should? *(She makes to rise.)*

MANUEL

No, no, we're safe here. Noisy bastards.

LUIS

Any of our lads turning up?

JESUS shrugs. It is possible.

DOLORES

Trouble?

EMILIA

Don't tell me I'm going to spoil me new dress!

JESUS

Of course not. This is a celebration. (*Lifts his glass.*)
Welcome back … Dolores … Manuel …

The noise is suddenly loud.

The sound of shots. They dive for cover.

PASIONARIA, in a doorway, is surprised to find MANUEL sliding
down beside her, blood pouring from his ear.

DOLORES

Manuel … ?

Light change.

ACT TWO – SCENE THREE

A meeting. JOSÉ, JESUS, LUIS and EMILIA wait for DOLORES in
silence. Pause.

LUIS

(*To EMILIA:*) How many from your area?

EMILIA

Two thousand. Probably more, it's … (*She shrugs,
unable to continue.*)

JESUS

(*Softly.*) Mother of God.

LUIS

And how many in jail?

EMILIA

Over thirty thousand in all ... again, we can't get
reliable figures.

JESUS

At least they're alive.

EMILIA

We've got reports of beatings and mutilation.

JOSÉ

How many? How many dead?

LUIS

(*Adding up on paper.*) Five thousand, two hundred
and six.

Silence.

JOSÉ

They want to murder every miner in Spain.

JESUS

Yes. They want to murder us.

EMILIA bursts out laughing. They gape at her.

JOSÉ

Funny?

EMILIA

What's the difference! You know what my man's doing
at this minute? Crawling ... three miles in and three
miles back, just to get to the coal face. His knees
aren't there anymore.

LUIS

You're lucky he's still got his balls. *(Throws her a newspaper. She reads the headlines and groans.)* They're sending in Arabs.

JOSÉ

Arabs?

LUIS

Arab mercenaries as strike-breakers, under this General Whatsisname.

JOSÉ

Another out of work killer from Morocco.

JESUS

They've found them something to do now.

LUIS

Yes. Finish us.

Together.

JESUS

Cut our legs off.

JOSÉ

How can they put us all in jail? Where's the coal coming from if we're not there to dig it up for them? Who's going to do it?

LUIS

We are.

JESUS

On our knees.

Slight pause.

EMILIA

My sister's husband's gone missing. And his brother.
We think they've gone across the border. Trouble is
we don't know.

LUIS

(As DOLORES arrives in a hurry.) Ah!

DOLORES

(Sits without ceremony.) Sorry I'm late.

LUIS

(To JESUS:) Take the chair?

EMILIA picks up pencil and paper to take the minutes.

JESUS

The situation is now critical. Five thousand miners
killed, strikes broken with the use of African troops,
whole villages burnt.

LUIS

At least we know where we are.

JESUS

We're here to vote on a course of action.

JOSÉ

What he means is, we're here to vote on a motion to
collaborate.

JESUS

It's a matter of practical politics.

JOSÉ

If we're seen to collaborate with socialists we're seen
to sell the revolution.

DOLORES

(*Quiet.*) Bugger the revolution. (*Shocked silence.
EMILIA draws in her breath audibly.*) If you mean by
revolution some sort of slop-bucket rubbish about a
clean sweep, then I say bugger the revolution because
it's going to murder the lot of us. What happens if we
don't collaborate?

JESUS

Without a Popular Front of the left, we haven't a hope
of governing ... ever.

DOLORES

The fascists are closing ranks. They have the Army,
the money. All we have are promises. We're an illegal
party, our numbers are minute. We've got no money
and half our people are in jail.

JESUS

(*To JOSÉ:*) As activists we'll have influence way
beyond our representation.

JOSÉ

Just because some of us are not prepared to stomach
a collaboration with ...

DOLORES

With any but the pure in heart? What are you, José,
some sort of idealist? Grow your hair and join the
anarchists.

JESUS

Come on, Dolores ...

DOLORES

We'll infiltrate. That suit you? (*She is suddenly
genial, knowing that she has won.*)

JOSÉ

It sickens me.

DOLORES

(*Sober.*) I know.

They stare at each other. Then he looks away.

A long pause.

JESUS

(*Softly.*) I propose the motion to co-opt.

Silence.

JESUS

Seconded?

LUIS nods. DOLORES and EMILIA raise their hands. They all wait.
At last JOSÉ, his face averted, raises his hand. Swift movement
at once as they all rise, putting on their coats and gathering their
belongings.

EMILIA crosses to DOLORES.

EMILIA

I've got the train tickets.

DOLORES

How many?

EMILIA

We're picking up two little boys ... five more at
Burgos ... (*Looks at list.*) Seven ... twenty-eight in all.
(*To JESUS;*) Women Against War – another ferrying
job. We're putting the kids out of the danger areas,
plus those whose parents are inside.

DOLORES mutters with rage.

EMILIA

(As they put their coats on.) Over five thousand now.
(No response from DOLORES.) Dead. Well?

DOLORES

(Snarls.) What do you want me to do – cry?

EMILIA looks at her, crosses to JOSÉ.

EMILIA

Hey, José, come and wipe the shit off your hands.

DOLORES makes to follow. JESUS breaks away from LUIS.

JESUS

Dolores. We want you to stand. As a Popular
Front candidate. *(She nods.)* You know what it
means?

DOLORES

Yes, I know. *(They all look at the ground.)*

JESUS

You'll have to give up ...

DOLORES

No! We've promised to get the kids out of it.

LUIS

Other people can do that.

DOLORES

No. Not just getting them somewhere safe ... it's
getting them to Madrid, walking the streets with
them ... shoving it under their noses. Miners
children, orphaned and bloody starving. We also have
to find homes – people who'll take them in.

LUIS

You could combine it with electioneering.

DOLORES

It is electioneering.

LUIS

Good. Then you're on? *(She nods and smiles. The TWO MEN exchange a smile.)*

DOLORES

What's up?

JESUS

We've got a surprise for you.

LUIS

We've found a school for your kids!

DOLORES

You haven't? Oh! Thank God. Where?

LUIS

In Moscow.

DOLORES

Moscow?

JESUS

They'll get a fine education!

LUIS

They'll be safe as houses, love.

DOLORES

You want me to send them to Russia?

LUIS

Got confirmation this morning.

JESUS

We didn't want to raise your hopes till we were sure.

LUIS

Lucky little devils!

DOLORES

You want me to give them up?

LUIS

God knows what's happening here, Dolores.

JESUS

If you campaign, they could be used against you as
hostages.

DOLORES

You want me to give up my children?

LUIS

Congratulations, love! (*Kisses her.*)

JESUS

You'll be free to work knowing they're safe. (*He
embraces her.*)

The TWO MEN go. DOLORES sings 'Safe.'

DOLORES

Well what are we given children
But to let them go?
They're not ours, like a cake tin,
The sooner we learn to do without them
The better.
Only
They're not ready,
They're not ready,
They're not ready.

Send them off with a smile …

It's their future!

You can see it in their eyes,

The excitement!

They're going on a train!

Do they realise they're not coming back?

Yes … but do they know what that means?

Can't you see,

They're not ready,

They're not ready,

They're not ready.

It's all for the best,

No more worries,

No more female irrelevant

Hampering of agenda.

Only …

They're not ready.

They're not ready.

They're not ready.

ACT TWO – SCENE FOUR

DOLORES and EMILIA, with TWO BOYS, wait for a train. The BOYS play about. TWO YOUNG SOLDIERS walk up and down, guarding the station.

EMILIA

(*Shouts to the SOLDIERS as they pass.*) How's it going?

ONE OF THE SOLDIERS turns, grins and waves.

The CHILDREN play. The SOLDIERS return.

EMILIA

What's going on ... anything?

SOLDIER ONE

No, not much.

DOLORES offers her cigarettes. They light up.

SOLDIER TWO

Seen anybody suspicious?

DOLORES

(Shouts to the BOYS.) Here, not so much noise!

EMILIA

(To SOLDIER.) Me? No. What are you here for? We're not all going to get raped, are we?

SOLDIER ONE

No such luck, missus. We're looking for this revolutionary Pasionaria.

EMILIA

Who?

SOLDIER TWO

We had word on the wire she come in on the ten o'clock this morning. *(He laughs as the FIRST SOLDIER plays football with the BOYS.)*

EMILIA

Is she dangerous?

SOLDIER ONE

(Calls as he punts the ball.) Only got fingernails six inches long!

SOLDIER TWO

They file 'em to a point. We been warned.

DOLORES

Coo, sounds nasty.

SOLDIER ONE

(*Returning.*) Don›t you worry, missus, we'll catch her.

SOLDIER TWO

We'll have her! (*Pats his rifle.*)

EMILIA

Be careful! Point the barrel down, son, for God's sake.

DOLORES

Shoot his bloody foot then. (*They smoke, watching
the CHILDREN.*)

SOLDIER TWO

Nice lads.

DOLORES

Yes.

SOLDIER TWO

Yours?

DOLORES

Mine? (*For a moment she is caught out, off guard.*)

EMILIA

No mine. Little devils. So, what's it like boys, army
life? (*She offers them food which they fall on
gratefully.*)

SOLDIER ONE

Rotten.

SOLDIER TWO

Can't complain.

DOLORES

(*Laughs.*) Make your minds up!

EMILIA

What made you join the army?

SOLDIER TWO

Out of work.

DOLORES

I hear there was bread riots here.

SOLDIER ONE

Yeah. Two killed.

EMILIA

Killed? Ooh Lord . . .

DOLORES

How did that happen then?

SOLDIER ONE

(*Chewing solidly.*) Had to fire in the crowd, didn't we?

DOLORES

(*Mildly, after a pause.*) You weren't worried?

SOLDIER ONE

Me? No!

DOLORES

I mean, firing on your own people.

EMILIA

(*Quick, worried at DOLORES' tone.*) Aren't you lads
supposed to be looking after us?

DOLORES

(*Genial.*) Yeah, come on, give the bosses a poke in the
eye for a change!

SOLDIER TWO

Yeah but they pay us, don't they?

SOLDIER ONE

Not the bloody mob. Get nothing out of them.

SOLDIER TWO

You don't like doing it.

SOLDIER ONE

It's the job. Obey orders and keep in with those on top.

SOLDIER TWO

We got to eat.

DOLORES

What if there's a civil war?

SOLDIER TWO

Have to fight, won't we?

DOLORES

Yeah but … I mean, wouldn't you be fighting your own families? *(She stands there frowning stupidly.)*

SOLDIER ONE

Never.

DOLORES

Yeah but, isn't that what it means, civil war? I thought it meant ordinary people like you and me against all the landlords. People that screw us down.

SOLDIER ONE

What are you, a communist or something?

DOLORES

No, it's just what they were on about in the café where I work.

SOLDIER ONE

Where's that then?

DOLORES

Oh Madrid. You get all sorts.

SOLDIER TWO

Big city eh?

EMILIA

Still . . . it makes sense.

SOLDIER ONE

Don't you believe it. Listen, we know what ticks. (*He walks off.*) God, you women get some silly ideas.

DOLORES

(*Living dangerously.*) So, you might have to join a war against your own class then?

EMILIA

(*Worried at this, diverts by calling to the CHILDREN.*) Hey, get down off there! Devils.

They laugh at the kids. The FIRST SOLDIER points his rifle at the KIDS, who put their hands up. ONE CHILD jumps on the SOLDIER'S back, the SOLDIER runs round with him.

DOLORES

You wouldn't do that, would you?

SOLDIER TWO

(*Laughing at the CHILDREN.*) What?

DOLORES

Fight against your own sort?

EMILIA

(*Fed up with DOLORES.*) Oh, bugger it!

SOLDIER TWO

I dunno, missus. Might have to. For a start, if we don't
do what we're told . . .

He makes an imitation of having his throat cut. They stand
together, smiling at the CHILDREN. The YOUNGER gets on the
SECOND SOLDIER'S back. He strolls with DOLORES, the CHILD on
his back.

SOLDIER TWO

My brother Claudio's all for this General Franco, the
one whose been beating up the miners up north. He
says he's a real good bloke. No nonsense. Really tough
bastard, so my brother says – real mean. Well . . .

The FIRST SOLDIER decants the CHILD and returns. He puts down
the BOY, and picks up his rifle.

SOLDIER TWO

It's what's needed. Thanks for the grub.

SOLDIER ONE

So long, girls! Keep your legs crossed.

DOLORES

So long, lads.

EMILIA

Here, wanna know something? She's Pasionaria!

SOLDIER TWO

Oh yeah? And I'm Greta Garbo!

SOLDIER ONE

Show us your fangs!

They laugh. The CHILDREN call 'Goodbye.' DOLORES watches
them go.

SOLDIER TWO

Cheerio!

EMILIA

Cheero, lads.

EMILIA takes the BOYS by the hands, for a stroll, and turns as
DOLORES makes a low sound, between a sigh and a moan.

EMILIA

What's up?

DOLORES

Nothing.

EMILIA

What is it?

DOLORES

Nothing.

EMILIA looks at her shrewdly, then exits with the two CHILDREN.
DOLORES gazes after the SOLDIERS.

DOLORES sings: 'My Sons.'

DOLORES

My sons . . .
Arms – legs – sinews -
All mine -
His eyes . . .
His eyes are running with blood!
Son, why are you bleeding?
My job to bleed, not yours.
Why are his nails rotting?
Where is his face?
"Only a few more weeks, Mother!"
Can you smell burning?

The meat is burning, Teresa.

There's no meat in the house.

My sons.

Why is your hair alight?

Where are your limbs?

"I'll be on leave soon, Mother,

Give us a smile."

This liver is tasty, goes well with the onions.

Juan? Juan! But I saw him -

There – in the doorway!

Who put this heart on the table?

Too small for an ox heart,

Too big for a lamb.

My sons-

Arms – legs – sinews

My flesh.

No-one consulted me.

Light change.

ACT TWO – SCENE FIVE

The voting box is set up. PEOPLE enter and vote.

The sound of cheering increases, off.

JESUS enters, a paper in his hand. He lifts an arm for silence.

JESUS

(His voice is on Tannoy.) The united parties of the left . . . the new, Popular Front . . . has, this day . . . been elected to the Cortes . . . to be the new government of our beloved Spain!

Deafening cheers and noise.

                    JESUS
     The results . . .

He cannot make himself heard for the cheering. He tries again.

                    JESUS
     The results . . . of the votes cast . . . read as follows . . .

Loud cheering and shouting.

                    JESUS
     A hundred and fifty-eight Republicans . . . eighty-eight
     socialists . . . seventeen communists . . . ten others . . .
     total . . . two hundred and seventy-three . . . *(Cheers)*.
     Total delegates from the right . . . two hundred and
     five!!

Cheers.

The sound of shots. The PEOPLE run off severally.

                                        Light change.

ACT TWO – SCENE SIX

The inner and outer gates of a prison.

DOLORES enters separately.

                    LUIS
     (Kissing DOLORES.) Congratulations!

                    JESUS
     Wonderful! Wonderful result! *(He shakes them both
     by the hand.*

Intermittent shouting and banging.

DOLORES

What's up here? (*She is full of the adrenalin of success.*)

LUIS

Riot. Prison Governor's lost control.

JESUS

They let us in yesterday.

LUIS

We've told them all. They're mostly political. We have to wait for the amnesty.

DOLORES

(*Yells above the noise.*) Can't we do nothing?

LUIS

(*Laughs, digs her in the ribs, yells.*) You're the Dep!

DOLORES

What?

JESUS

(*Smiles.*) You're the Deputy.

DOLORES

I am. Right. Let's have the little man with the wobbly knees in.

LUIS exits, returns with the MAYOR.

MAYOR

For God's sake do something, they'll kill us all!

EMILIA

Who's this!

MAYOR

(*Affronted.*) I am the Mayor of this city! Which one of you gentlemen is the Deputy?

DOLORES

I'm the Deputy.

The MAYOR gives her a brief, puzzled glance, and turns to the MEN.

DOLORES

I said ... I'm the Deputy.

The MAYOR is shocked.

DOLORES

Yes. Me.

MAYOR

You? You're a woman!

EMILIA

That's right.

MAYOR

But ... she's just a peasant woman!

DOLORES

That's right.

He gibbers.

DOLORES

Now listen. I want you to call off your civil guard, and let these men out.

MAYOR

What?

LUIS

Dolores, I'm afraid you can't ...

DOLORES

You heard me. Let them out.

MAYOR

(Faint.) On whose authority?

JESUS

(To DOLORES:) Dolores, we must be seen to abide by the law.

DOLORES

(To the MAYOR:) How many men have you got?

MAYOR

Eleven.

DOLORES

Armed?

MAYOR

Yes.

DOLORES

Get them in here.

JESUS

Pasionaria . . . hold on, do consider . . .

MAYOR

Pasionaria?!

They help him to sit.

LUIS

(Urgent.) Jesus is right. You've just been elected. If the first action you're seen to take is breaking the law . . .

DOLORES

(*Snarls, turning on him.*) Breaking the law? Listen!
(*As the noise becomes deafening.*) the people of
Asturias voted for us on the promise of liberty
for all political prisoners. All right! We let a few
rogues out as well. D'you think that maggot and
his whey-faced cowpats are going to hold that gate
much longer? We might as well do the right thing,
let them out and get the credit for it! Where are the
keys?

EMILIA

Go it, gal!

PRISONERS appear at the inner door, shouting. TWO GUARDS
appear at the outer door, with guns. DOLORES springs forward.

DOLORES

Oh Christ, they're going to shoot. Get back! The
bastards are going to shoot!

She leaps on the outer gate and climbs over to join the
PRISONERS. ONE OF THE GUARDS pushes out LUIS, JESUS and
EMILIA.

The MAYOR runs off.

PRISONERS

Mind out, gal. That's it!

They cheer her.

PRISONER ONE

Out of the way, Pash.

PRISONER TWO

We're going to rush the gates!

DOLORES

They've got guns!

The PRISONERS rush the inner door, unsuccessfully.

The TWO GUARDS appear with their guns.

DOLORES

Christ, they're going to kill us!

The GUARDS stand off. The PRISONERS subside.

PRISONER ONE

You're one of us now, Dolores.

PRISONER THREE

She's an old con!

VOICE

Pasionaria – Pasionaria, will you come out please?

DOLORES

(*Calls.*) I'll come out when we all come out!

The MEN cheer.

DOLORES

My God, I thought they were going to kill the lot of us!

PRISONER TWO

Give you a scare, eh?

DOLORES

Not half.

PRISONER THREE

Is it true then? Are you in the government?

DOLORES

Yes. Any questions?

PRISONER TWO

I don't believe it! (*He whoops, throws his cap in the air.*)

PRISONER ONE

(*To DOLORES, as a challenge.*) Now what?

DOLORES

(*Calls.*) Send in the Mayor!

The MAYOR enters, trembling. They jeer.

DOLORES

Well, what's the verdict?

MAYOR

No-one has authority to give permission. The prison governor is willing to convene a meeting . . .

DOLORES

Give me the keys. As Deputy for Asturias I take full responsibility for the release of all prisoners.

MAYOR

I can't.

DOLORES

Give me the keys.

MAYOR

There are common criminals in there!

DOLORES

Too bad.

She holds out her hand. Pause. He gives her the keys and she unlocks the door.

Celebration.

Light change.

ACT TWO – SCENE SEVEN

The PRIME MINISTER at his desk. A SECRETARY enters.

SECRETARY

Prime Minister ... His Honour the Deputy from
Navarre ... Senor Jesus Murillo.

The PRIME MINISTER rises, embraces JESUS.

JESUS

Prime Minister, I've urgent news.

PM

Coffee?

JESUS

No thank you. I'm sorry to bring ...

PM

You won't mind if I do. (*He rings the bell. The
SECRETARY enters.*) Coffee for one, sure you won't
change your mind?

The SECRETARY goes.

JESUS

The situation in Navarre is serious. The area's becoming
an armed fortress ... guns flooding across the border ...

PM

Oh come! We've had reports ... a few hotheads
dragging rifles through the bushes ...

JESUS

No, these people are disciplined. They're forming
private armies. Everywhere I went I saw drilling,
manoeuvres, target practice, all quite open.

PM

But that's illegal!

JESUS

Foreign licence plates everywhere, arms dealers,
Germans swilling beer in the cafes. I tell you, the
scum of Europe's flooding in.

PM

Navarre's always been a trouble spot.

JESUS

It's gone beyond that. (*He places photographs before
the PRIME MINISTER.*) There's been widespread
intimidation – people beaten up – whole villages have
been destroyed.

PM

Ye-es, ugly. We Spanish, we're a passionate people,
Jesus. Give them a by-election, feelings run high ...

JESUS

The whole area is seceding. Come and see for yourself.

PM

Nothing I'd like more. A trip out of Madrid, away from
this desk. You know, I envy you chaps.

JESUS

Can't I get it into your thick head? Navarre is in
a state of armed resistance! The Fascists are in
control!

PM

Now that's enough! You see Fascists behind every
bush. You're as much to blame.

JESUS

Read the facts! The facts!

The PM hits the bell. The SECRETARY enters with coffee.

PM

My dear chap, calm down.

JESUS

People are being killed – innocent people!

PM

It'll be looked into. Now Jesus, my old friend, get some rest.

JESUS

I am not fatigued, nor am I being hysterical, Prime Minister. The matter is urgent.

PM

Yes, yes, I understand. I'll look into it. You're a good fellow – you're all good fellows. Rest assured . . .

JESUS

If you will just read the report. The pictures speak for themselves!

PM

(Ushering him out.) It'll be attended to. (He drinks coffee. The SECRETARY places papers before him, one at a time.) My God . . . down again?

SECRETARY

I'm afraid the money's pouring out of this country.

PM

We must make some arrests as an example. I had to stop my own sister-in-law speculating. What's this?

SECRETARY

Telegram, sir. (*He reads*) 'Valencia Falangists have
seized radio station and broadcast the following:
'The military forces of the Falange occupy this radio
station. Greetings to our followers and to all patriotic
Spaniards everywhere."

PM

Are they still there?

SECRETARY

No, they cut the telegraph wires and left.

PM

But they can't do that, it's illegal! How are we
supposed to get through?

SECRETARY

The governor is on the line. He's asking for
instructions.

PM

Oh, tell him to play the National Anthem, and
broadcast a speech – prank storm in a teacup, that
sort of thing. And tell him to call for calm. We mustn't
inflame the situation whatever happens – that's how
trouble starts.

JESUS

But . . .

PM

Our job is to keep the peace, not drive ourselves into
war!

Light change.

<u>ACT TWO – SCENE EIGHT</u>

Rival placards and banners are carried across the stage.

Enter JESUS and DOLORES. She hands him a paper.

> JESUS
>
> (*Reads, muttering first, then aloud.*) ' … the
> political and labour organisation represented by
> the undersigned offer the government their full
> support … '

> DOLORES
>
> (*Over his shoulder:*) ' … to strengthen the Popular
> Front, now in danger from enemies of the Republic.
> Signed Santiago Carrillo, José Diaz.

> JESUS
>
> If it comes to a fight, what have we …

> DOLORES
>
> But if we stick …

> JESUS
>
> I know. (*He looks at her sadly.*) At least your children
> are safe.

> DOLORES
>
> You think it'll … (*She turns away.*) It's true. I couldn't
> bear it if …

They stand apart, each deep in thought.

> DOLORES
>
> The survival of this Republic – democratically
> elected, seen by the whole world – its survival affects
> everything! (*Pause.*) You think it's over, don't you?

JESUS

What I think ... What I want to believe, and what I
feel ...

DOLORES

We're going to win this debate. We're going to get a
full vote of confidence from the House.

But he looks at her, a long look.

DOLORES

Even if ...

Pause.

JESUS

If it came to civil war, I'd kill myself.

DOLORES

(Slight pause.) Don't even think about it. What we've
achieved! Our success – it's indelible. Progress isn't
continuous – Jesus, you know that. It goes in waves.
We have to think ahead. What we do now matters so
much – for the future ... however things ... whatever
happens to us ... *(Pause.)* We have to concentrate
on international support, political and financial. It
must happen, and there must be enough of it. There
must! We've arranged full press coverage as soon as
the debate is over. Exposure. You'll see! I've got the
world's press out there drinking us dry!

She makes him laugh. He embraces her again and goes.

Alone, DOLORES walks. Now her own fears invade her. She pauses,
and leans her back against the wall, trying to see the future.

Light change.

ACT TWO – SCENE NINE

In Parliament.

Available members of the cast as DEPUTIES are ranged separately to indicate party bias.

SENOR MONTALBAN

> I propose the motion: that the opposition, on behalf of the people of this country, ask the government to explain the reasons for the subversive state in which our beloved Spain now finds herself.

Loud cries of 'No!' – and noises of dissent from the government benches.

MONTALBAN

> Since the election of the Popular Front, there has been grave and increasing unrest throughout the country. Strikes … stoppages … whole villages laying down their tools. There have been repeated clashes with the forces of law and order, deploying valuable manpower and bleeding national resources. It is not, and it never has been, our intention to destroy the Popular Front. We don't need to. They are destroying themselves. (*Noise.*) Yes, you can shout! Look at them! What sort of government represents us? Who speaks in our name? We have a government composed of socialists … anarchists … even communists, whose allegiance is not to Spain at all but to a foreign power – to Russia! And, I might add, what's been happening there recently, eh? Purges, despotism, destruction! My friends, the situation is grave. The future of our great and historic country is at risk. Spain falters. Until … and unless … we

see vital and immediate change. Why then, I must
tell you that this government will preside over the
funeral of democracy.

Cheers and shouts.

Calls to the PRIME MINISTER to answer. Reluctantly he rises to
his feet.

> PM
>
> Gentlemen ... *(He tries to quell the noise.)* ...
> honourable gentlemen. Gentlemen, remember where
> you are! Your courtesy please! Gentlemen!

He waits for silence.

> PM
>
> I ask the chamber's forgiveness, but, despite his
> eminence as a statesman, I must honestly say that
> I disagree with the Honourable Senor. There are
> not many who can match his eloquence ... *(Shouts
> of agreement.)* ... nonetheless ... nevertheless ... I
> must try to put the situation into perspective. Spain
> is at the crossroads. We are at a turning of the ways.
> The people have voted ... *(Noise begins again.)* ...
> The people have voted for a government whose only
> wish is to see the prosperity of every man, woman
> and child assured. There is nothing we will not do, no
> sacrifice we are not prepared to undertake ...

> FERNANDEZ
>
> Oh, sit down!

> PM
>
> ... to ensure the well-being, not of a section, or any
> one class ...

FERNANDEZ

Sit down!

A chorus of 'Sit down's.' The noise rises. The PRIME MINISTER
throws up his hands and sits.

JESUS leans down, and whispers to the PRIME MINISTER.

The PRIME MINISTER looks up and back at DOLORES. She comes
down to his side for a brief conversation as the noise becomes
deafening.

FERNANDEZ

Look what we're up against? Look at him! They
can't even get men. They're hiding behind women's
skirts now! Get back behind the counter, and leave
government to those bred for it – fit for it! All right
when they were promising the idiot peasantry the
moon eh? Telling them fair shares for all! They want
their manor houses, do they? Their palaces? They
want to live like hidalgos – like dukes – princes – is
that it? Without the wherewithal? Well, I'm very
sorry. I'm sorry. I'm sorry to have to tell the people
of this country . . . or of any country . . . never mind
all the weak and wet do-gooders, and all the coat-
tail jackals of the left – you can't have it! Christmas
is over this year! No free gifts! Look at me. Look at
me. I'm a self-made man, and proud of it. Hard work!
Common Sense! Persistence and sobriety! That's
what made me. Made me what I am. (Cheers from the
Right.) And prayer. And prayer! I'm not ashamed to
admit, admit – freely – that every morning I get down
on my hands and knees and I give thanks, and ask
the odd favour from He who in His Mightiness can
grant it. But I don't expect something for nothing.

I expect to Work ... Work! (*Noise.*) What's wrong
with it, you lazy buggers? Better than waiting for
handouts ... for somebody else to get it for you while
you sit on your backsides in envy and idleness. I had
six hundred workers in my factory ...

VOICE
We know all about your workers, and what you paid
them!

FERNANDEZ
Six hundred! Before I gave it all over to my son and
came into parliament for a tenth of the income I was
making. Six hundred wage packets! Don't talk to
me about work. I know what I'm talking about. The
unions understand me. We understand each other.
The working man wants work, not interference
with his livelihood. If we go down, he goes down. He
understands that. He's not the fool you think. Sooner
or later, it hits the pocket ... and people see sense.
They want that wage in their hands from those who
can get it for them. No messing. Promises of fair
play – can you buy bread with promises? This isn't
the school playground! People want to eat! They want
a roof over their head and pesetas in their pockets!
You talk about a fuller life? You can talk for the rest
of your life, you won't achieve it. There's only one
thing that'll achieve that for you, for me, for any man.
Money! Money! Payment. Life costs! Back to reality,
I say. Forget the daydreams we've been fed since this
liquorice assortment tricked the electorate. Sanity
is beginning to reign. The people are realising. Even
the miners in the north are coming to heel. It's one
thing to want to get out of dirty, dangerous work,

to want something better for your children … but
when the seams start running out – oh dear – help –
what's going to happen to our livelihoods? They can't
get down there quick enough. They're grateful for
anything – and so they should be! So should you all
be! Use your heads! That's my message to the people
of this country. We all know what's going to happen
next. We know what's coming. And we know, those
of us who have any sense, the necessity for it. The
Spanish people will not tolerate the continuance of
disorder. I call upon every man of sanity in this house
to vote Yes! to the motion. Law and Order for Spain!
(*Noise.*) Law and Order will be restored!!

He sits, to cheers and boos. DOLORES rises. Silence.

DOLORES

(*Quietly.*) These are manoeuvres. These manoeuvres
by the Right haven't ceased since we took office.
It wasn't the Popular Front which took a national
decision to lower workers' wages. It was, at the
urgent request of the opposition, the industrialists.
It wasn't the Popular Front who set the Civil Guard
on starving peasants, who'd see harvests rotting on
the stalk rather than negotiate wages – because a
settlement meant popularity for this government. If
Senor Robles wants to know why villagers obediently
downed tools, I'll tell him. Because their houses were
burnt when they refused. It wasn't the Popular Front
who refused to meet workers' organisations. Nor was
it the Popular Front who sent armed mercenaries to
assassinate men of democratic principle …

Uproar. She shouts above it.

DOLORES

The good faith of this government is being slandered
by the very elements of disorder! This government is
under attack. This government is the people of Spain.
It is the people of Spain who are under attack.

More uproar. She waits for quiet.

DOLORES

And we are vulnerable. Oh yes. The people of Spain,
and their government, are truly vulnerable to your
depredations. Why? Because previous, reactionary
governments have created such sustained misery
for the vast majority of the people of this country
that we, the Republican government, have to change
everything. The land is still in the hands of the
few. It's more economic to farm in large units, we're
told ... this is the modern method. But we have
nineteen million untouched acres. Land left for the
sport of the few. What is more, we see, when we look
abroad at these new, economic ventures, that they
overproduce. That they're a mess of glut and subsidy,
that there is no sense in the way they carry on –
except, of course, in terms of greed and exploitation.
The forests, the fields, the factories ... the towns, the
villages ... all, still, in the hands of the reactionaries.
Whose aim is simple, and united. Oh, how they parade
their unity! To hang on to what they have stolen. For
greed ... and for power. It is this power that we have
to take away. Mark my words, we have to take it.
Leeches won't fall off your back for the asking. Rats
won't leave for a bow ... not even, Senor Casares. (She
turns to him with an ironic bow) ... not even if you
put on a fancy hat and squeak for them! No, you can't

expect fleas, lice, leeches, rats not to hang on. It is
their nature. The people of Spain have a cunning and
vicious enemy.

Uproar.

DOLORES

You think I exaggerate? Then listen to the talk
within these walls … the deals … the 'realistic'
appraisals. The cynicism of the right is total. How
can that man stand there and sneer at the miners of
this country? You are talking about people's lives!
He sneers, because faced with starvation, a man
begs to crawl underground and cough his lungs out,
in order to feed his family. He sneers … He sneers
and he is exultant to have men so cowed. He calls
them 'realistic.' Do we really believe we can be fairly
governed by such people? People who will empty the
coffers of Spain if the interest rate is right? You call
that patriotism? Oh, but they tell us, let us make the
money, we who know how. Leave it to us – we, the
privileged, the educated. What can you do without
us? Where are your schools, your hospitals, your
fancy ideas without the money we make? What do we
see you do with the money you make? Never mind
what you say … what do we see you do? You eat our
flesh, and you drink our blood. Not acceptable. You
think we want to be like you? You are not acceptable.
Unacceptable. We can't afford you. Not while a child
on this earth goes hungry. Who are the true enemies
of this country? Of any country? I say they are those
who erode the freedoms of the people. Those who
contemptuously believe that the people can be bullied
and bribed into submission. Those who believe that

the people – the people – have no voice, no rights. No
say in their own lives. Do you know what I say? I say
we should imprison those who destroy the livelihoods
of others. I say we should condemn those who rule
only for gain – who believe personal betterment to
be a worthy human aspiration. You over there ... can
you not see that a morality of human decency is our
only code for survival? No government is perfect.
Government is people – we are not perfect. But,
however imperfectly, we – the Popular Front – speak
for the people of this country. All the people – yes,
even you lot! What do you do? You sit there grinning
and trying to destroy us. By whose authority?
On whose behalf? Let me ask you this. *(She leans
forward.)* Who, as representatives paid by the people,
are you governing for? Who are you governing for?
WHO ARE YOU GOVERNING FOR?

Blackout.

The End.

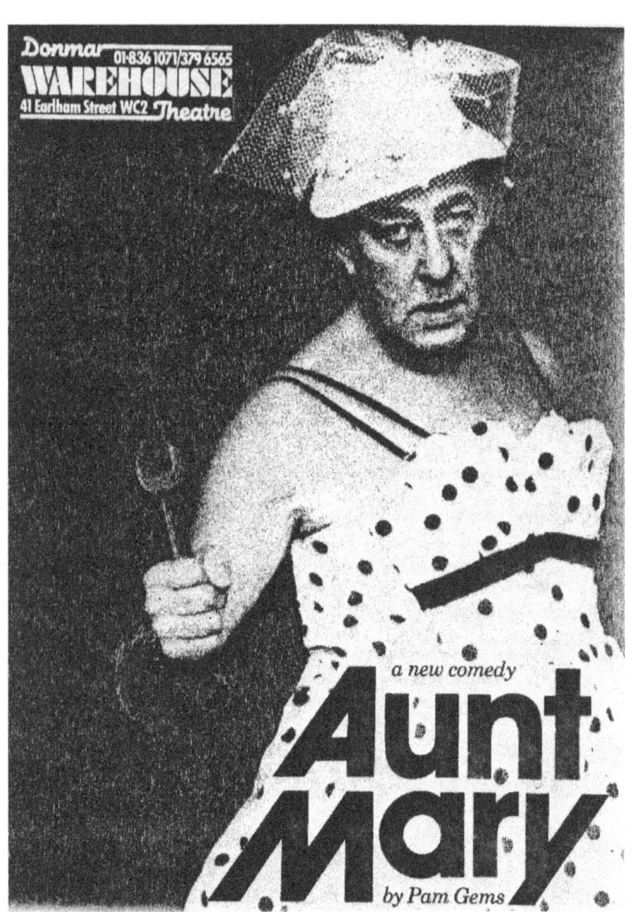

Donmar
WAREHOUSE
41 Earlham Street WC2 Theatre
01-836 1071/379 6565
a new comedy
Aunt Mary
by Pam Gems

AUNT MARY

SCENES FROM PROVINCIAL LIFE

For Timothy Spall

FOREWORD

Pam Gems didn't write about herself. She wrote to escape. Much as when we go to the theatre, we also seek escape.

Like many of us, she was traumatised in childhood. But she was doubly traumatised by going straight from the frying pan of childhood into the fire of the Second World War.

'Stiff upper lip.' That's what they called it. Stiff Upper Lip: the British way of dealing with trauma, which meant denial and diversion into humour. This quintessentially British trait is succinctly personified by the Black Knight in *Monty Python and the Holy Grail*.

When the Black Knight's arm is cut off, he says: "'Tis but a scratch."

King Arthur (shocked): A scratch? Your arm's off!

Black Knight: No, it isn't.

King Arthur indicates the Black Knight's arm lying on the ground.

King Arthur: What's that then?

Black Knight: I've had worse.

Pam Gems rarely wrote about herself. Nor did she often speak about herself. When she did, she invariably made things up, or gave them a fanciful spin. Her husband, Keith Gems was the same. A traumatic childhood, raised by a mother who dressed him as a girl and called him Shirley, and was frequently admitted to the Whitecroft mental asylum. Keith spent four years commanding air-sea rescue boats during the war but refused to speak about it.

Writing about yourself is therapeutic but – for some – revisiting old traumas is too much to bear. It's easier to forget them. Moreover, when you write about yourself, you run the risk of producing material that's only of interest to you.

The dissociative impulse, which powered Pam's extraordinary output, refashioned her concerns into other worlds and other characters. Her need to staunch her own wounds migrated to attempting to heal the wounds of others. She was a wounded healer.

AUNT MARY, although packaged in fantasy, is a rare item in her oeuvre, being fearlessly autobiographical. Her first stage-play, *Betty's Wonderful Christmas*, begins autobiographically but soon dissociates. Another autobiographical piece is *Finchie's War*, but this, too, is spun in a mist of anodized nostalgia. Autobiographical elements can be seen peeping through in *Arthur and Guinevere*, *Natalya*, *The Socialists*, and *At The Window*, but *Aunt Mary* is the only play where we hear Pam speaking in her own voice.

Pam's voice is in both Aunt Mary and Cyst, who exhibit the masculine and feminine sides of her nature. The other characters are satirical sketches of some of her own dysfunctional family. Jack is her husband, Keith. Martin is me. I was shocked, when I saw the play, to hear things I'd said to Pam coming out of Martin's mouth. It felt like I was being undressed in public. Muriel is Pam's mother, Elsie, mixed with the innocent sweetness of Pam's Down's Syndrome daughter, Lala.

Alison, the TV presenter, represents The Business, which Pam saw as the enemy. In her view, the entertainment business corrupts art and artists by exploiting them for money and status. This was, for Pam, a painful, personal issue, with which she wrestled all her writing life.

After working for the BBC for several years in audience research, Pam acquired an aversion to that august institution later intensified by their conceited, ham-fisted treatment of her – and of other writers and actors.

The philistine nature of the BBC existed also, to a lesser

extent, in subsidized theatre. The Arts Council of Great Britain was run by the same brainwashed and entitled, Oxford and Cambridge graduates that managed the BBC.

Pam Gems's dream was to own a small, independent theatre (as in the play) where ideas could flourish free from political correctness and perception management.

Her other dream was for her family to, somehow, find a harmonious way to co-exist.

Jonathan Gems

AUNT MARY was first performed at the Donmar Warehouse, Covent Garden, London, UK, on the 15th June, 1982, with the following cast.

CAST

Muriel	ANNE WAY
Martin	TIMOTHY SPALL
Mary	ALFRED MARKS
Cyst	BARRY JACKSON
Jack	PETER ATTARD
Alison	PATRICIA QUINN

Director	ROBERT WALKER
Designer	DAVID FIELDING
Lighting	CHARLIE PATON
Stage Manager	DAVID PROCTOR
Deputy Stage Manager	CHARLOTTE WARNER
Assistant Stage Manager	PETER STONE

Produced by Omega Productions

AUNT MARY

SCENES FROM PROVINCIAL LIFE

<u>ACT ONE – SCENE ONE</u>

The forecourt of a petrol station.

Up right is a café, practical inside, ditto balcony above, with two separate signs which read 'CAFÉ' and 'THEATRE' ... the second with a direction arrow.

Down-right is a round table painted dark green, park chairs, and a triple swing seat decorated and swagged with cushions in inky damask, and a silk shawl. Down centre and left are two pumps, air-pipe, a stack of tyres, a plastic bucket, and a large roll of blue paper on a stand. A wooden bench is under a large rose-tree, in bloom.

Up left is an ornamental pond in the Japanese style, appointed with stones, sand and a willow tree.

A sunlit midsummer afternoon. The MUSIC of Jimmy Yancey's 'South Side Stuff.'

MUSIC held, then down to crossfade the sound of a lark. Pause.

Enter MURIEL. She wears a chiffon scarf over her hair. She is small and elderly.

MURIEL

Cooee ... anybody in?

JACK

(*From within.*) Muriel?

MURIEL

Jack? I've come for my shampoo and set.

She goes inside. Pause.

MARTIN enters from down right. He is young, wears a white shirt, carries a guitar and an old rucksack. He goes into the café, helps himself to a beer, comes out, drinking from the can. He sits at the table and writes.

The sound of a lark.

CYST crosses, up left, from the garden. He wears a pale wig and a tulle dress in sweet-pea colours. He makes to go indoors when MARTIN looks up.

MARTIN

Hi, Cyst.

CYST is startled. He gives a small scream.

CYST

(Southern Belle accent.) Why, Martin . . . .hello.
Please don't get up, I'm only passing through.

MARTIN

Blanche?

CYST

(Little curtsey. From behind his fan.) Why thank you,
kind sir. My it's hot.

MARTIN

It's the humidity.

CYST

(Slipping into North Country.) Do what?

MARTIN

The humidity. It makes you sweat.

CYST

(*Shy laugh.*) Oh. Don't let me stop you.

MARTIN

(*Puts his pen down.*) It's okay. I've finished.

CYST

D'you want to read it?

MARTIN

Later. When Mary's here.

CYST

(*Offended.*) Suit yourself.

MARTIN

He's not so critical!

CYST

Mary? Not critical?

MARTIN

You're worse. You tell the truth.

CYST

I do not. Any road, don't listen to me, I got off at the Georgians. It was all that horrible war ... the end of poetry, all ground to sludge on Flanders field.

MARTIN

T.S. Eliot? Ezra Pound?

CYST

(*Scornful.*) Imagists!

MARY enters with a silver tea-tray set with tea things. He is fortyish, good-looking, and wears a T-shirt and sarong and sandals.

MARY

Hi kid.

MARTIN

Hi Mary.

MARY

Good gig? *(Puts a huge club sandwich before MARTIN.)*

CYST

What?

MARTIN

Poetry fest. Nah. *(He eats ravenously.)* All verse, no poetry.

MARY

So, go with the flow.

CYST

(Glares at him.) Art for art's sake! *(He proffers a beautiful cake.)*

MARTIN

Wow!

MARY

Our new recipe from Jamaica.

He cuts MARTIN a huge slice. They stand over him as he tastes, and closes his eyes in bliss.

MARTIN

Wowee!

MARY pours tea, placated.

MARTIN

(Mouth full.) Why don't you like the Imagists, Cyst?

CYST shrugs, dismissive.

CYST

Trying to be obscure is vulgar. Auden called it swank.

MARTIN

He can talk.

MARY puts down a cup of tea for MARTIN.

MARY

Auden ... is as clear as crystal, as sound as a bell.
(*As CYST winces.*) Sorry about the clichés, lover.

CYST

I had noticed "go with the flow."

They drink and eat.

MARTIN

How was your trip to Jamaica?

CYST

Oh Martin! Birds like insects ... insects like birds ...
big climbing sticky things coming in at you through
the window ...

MARY

Shut up, you're making a fool of yourself.

CYST

He was sick. Both ways. All over his shoes and all
over ...

MARY

Thank you. Where's Muriel? (*He calls, loud.*) Muriel?

CYST

Jack's putting her under the drier.

                    MARY

Well, keep him away from the washbasin. It was the
kiss of life last time.

                    MARTIN

Jack okay?

                    MARY

Sure.

                    MARTIN

Still on remand?

                    MARY

Charges dropped. Lack of evidence.

                    MARTIN

Did he do it?

                    MARY

You kidding? I've got forty brace of pheasant in that
freezer.

JACK enters. He is young, and looks villainous in black vest and
trousers.

                    JACK

Tea up? *(To MARTIN.)* Hi – oh, great!

He grabs most of the sandwiches ... hoists the guitar.

                    JACK

Okay?

                    MARTIN

Sure.

JACK goes to exit.

                    JACK

Beer anyone?

MARY scowls. JACK exits.

> MURIEL
>
> (*From above, fanning herself with her magazine.*)
> Ooh dear!

> MARY
>
> Cyst tell you we're writing an opera?

> MARTIN
>
> No, what about?

> CYST
>
> John Ruskin.

> MARTIN
>
> Being upset about his wife having pubic hair?

> MARY
>
> (*Irritable.*) For fuck's sake.

> MARTIN
>
> What happens?

> MARY
>
> Not a lot.

> CYST
>
> We've got a good baritone for Ruskin ...

> MARY
>
> ... spade from Handsworth.

> CYST
>
> There's a walk-on for you if you're free, Martin.

> MARY
>
> Monsieur Sardine, the embalmer.

> MARTIN
>
> Thanks.

MURIEL

(*From above.*) Ohh! Oh dear!

MARY

You okay, Muriel?

MURIEL

Almost!

CYST

(*Screeches.*) Carolle, you're going on fire!

MARY

I knew it ... I knew it ... !

He and MARTIN rush off. CYST is left, transfixed with shock.

CYST

Oh Carolle ... oh!

MURIEL is brought out and they hose her down.

MARY

You all right, babes?

MURIEL

Rather windswept, Mary.

CYST sits MURIEL down.

MARY

I'll kill that cunt.

MARTIN

(*Putting a cushion behind her.*) OK, Muriel?

CYST

It's not Muriel, it's Carolle.

MURIEL

I've changed my name. Muriel dates me, don't you
think?

MARTIN

Who chose Carolle?

CYST

Don't you like it?

MARTIN

No.

MURIEL

(*Wistfully.*) I did think of Hortense.

MARTIN opens his mouth to object to that too.

MARY

Read your poem.

MARTIN reaches into his pocket, brings out his notebook. He reads

MARTIN
Pillow of muscat and pomegranate.
What's been done has been done,
Achieved,
Has been said,
Is said,
Is being said.
Or so you think.
Attica irises,
Fork-fringed, sea-wired on the pillow.
She has island eyes, this girl.
Purely by accident I look sideways.
Splinters.
What's all this?
Why the jet-propelled missiles

Homing in,
Their escorts quivering in the walls?
What, in the fragments of micro-
processed plexiglas,
Has been going on?

It's not finished of course. What do you think?
Mary?

MARY

Sex and passion, sex and passion.

MARTIN

What else is there?

MURIEL

Birds?

MARTIN

There's more to life than poultry, Muriel.

MURIEL

In a way.

She shivers suddenly. CYST takes her inside. The sound of a
Beethoven slow movement as CYST switches it on in the house.

MARY

You're right, kid. Don't waste a minute of it. Not a
drop.

MARTIN

I do think about sex – a lot. And words of course.

He gets up – looks out at the view. He turns.

MARTIN

Mary – that woman I was telling you about . . .

MARY

Face of an angel? Loins of a fox?

MARTIN

That's the one. She's working at Pebble Mill. Wants to come and pick me up. Okay with you?

MARY

Sure, if she's good-looking.

MARTIN, happy, leaps towards the door. And stops.

MARY

What?

MARTIN

Nothing. (*Turns to go. And back.*) Look, ah, it's just – ah – no, it's fine.

He goes inside. MARY rises, looks out at the view, wanders off.

The lights lower to twilight. Lights on, severally, within. The porch and forecourt lights go on.

MUSIC: Jimmy Yancey's 'At the Window.'

ALISON appears. She is very attractive, casually dressed. She pauses, not knowing her way. She crosses to door, knocks, listens, knocks again. She feels warm, lifts the hair from her neck, crosses to the pond. Takes off her shoes, and goes in for a paddle.

MARY, sinister in a black silk suit and polo neck, stands in the dark, enjoying his cigar.

ALISON plays prettily. Refreshed, she emerges from the pool. MARY grabs her. ALISON shrieks.

MUSIC out.

MARY

Hey, baby . . .

ALISON

Get off, get off me! Who the hell are you?

MARY

Say hullo to your Aunt Mary!

Light change.

ACT ONE – SCENE TWO

The next morning.

CYST and MARY are reading the Sunday papers.

JACK, apart, turns the pages of a paperback rapidly, splitting the spine. He makes sounds of enjoyment, which irritates MARY.

MARTIN suns himself, hat over his face, reading.

ALISON enters, leans over JACK to see what he is reading.

ALISON

Oh, Lily de Winter!

CYST looks up. ALISON smiles.

ALISON

Good morning. Have you finished with this?

She picks up a supplement and sits, displaying her legs and distracting MARY.

CYST

You saw the pictures of Irek?

MARY

Who?

CYST

(*Ratty.*) Mukhamedov – the ballet!

JACK

Caw . . . ooaw!

MARY

Jack?

JACK

What?

MARY

Shut up.

Silence as they all read.

JACK

Ah fuck. (*He throws the book away.*)

CYST

What's the matter?

JACK

She didn't get it. He didn't give it to her!

CYST picks up the book, smooths it gently, and stands over JACK.

CYST

Jack, they have to be married. (*He finds the last page, reads.*) Lady Veronica says to him "Hugo – we have the whole of our lives ahead. Let's not spoil things."

JACK

I don't get it. He wants it, she wants it . . .

CYST

Jack . . . society is a structure . . .

JACK

Yeah?

CYST

... as a leaf is a structure ... the design of a moth's
wing is a structure ...

MARY, rattling his paper, looks up.

MARY

He means you're not supposed to come on all the
time!

JACK

How're you supposed to get it, then?

MARY

(*Shrugs.*) Ask the lady.

ALISON

(*Thinks, then*) Gentle persistence? Sensational
presents? (*Returns to her supplement.*)

CYST

The world loves a gentleman, Jack.

JACK

Right. (*Belches delicately.*) Oops, beg pardon.

ALISON masks a smile.

CYST

Probably that marrow. It's never good to eat on an
empty stomach.

MARY rises. ALISON intervenes smoothly.

ALISON

Martin tells me you write.

MARY smiles but does not answer.

ALISON

I'm interested. My line of country.

MARY

Yuh?

CYST

It says here there's a new ointment, Mary. (*He licks his finger, turns a page.*) Probably no good for your piles.

MARY looks dangerous.

ALISON

(*Quickly.*) Are you published?

JACK

You bet! (*He gets a warning look from MARY.*)

ALISON

Who with?

MARY

We cover the waterfront.

CYST groans at the cliché.

ALISON

How do you mean?

JACK

They write under different names. (*Now CYST hisses at him.*)

ALISON

You both write?

There is no response.

ALISON

Interesting.

JACK

(*Picks up the book he was reading.*) This is one of
Cyst's.

ALISON

Lily de Winter? But she's adorable!

CYST

(*Flutters and then says wickedly.*) There's a collection
of Jeff Sprague indoors if you're interested.

ALISON

All that macho heavy-metal? No thanks.

JACK

Mary's.

ALISON

Oh. Sorry.

MARY shrugs amiably.

ALISON

Who else? I'm dying to know.

JACK

(*Pointing at MARY and CYST in turn.*) They are Jeff
Sprague, William Girdle, Moira Parkin, Bill Spruce,
Olivia Warner ... and Lily de Winter.

MARY

Jack, shut your mouth.

ALISON

What? All of them? (*To CYST.*) Moira? You? I love
that fey Irish colleen! And Girdle's wonderful saga.
(*Remembers the name.*) God's Annexe! I sat up all
night! You're having me on.

MARY

Sure, babes.

ALISON looks from him to JACK and then to CYST – who is agitated.

ALISON

(*Thoughtfully.*) We tried to get Bill Spruce for Arts
Ahoy but he was in Siberia.

JACK laughs.

ALISON

And Moira? What was it when we tried to reach her?
(*She tries to remember*) They said she'd – she'd ...

MARTIN

Joined the Little Sisters of Lazio. (*Getting up.*)
Bacon sandwich?

ALISON

Wicked. (*As MARTIN goes inside.*) I'm sorry, I don't
get it. Why the pseudonyms? Are you on the run or
something?

JACK

No! All kosher. They use their own names here, in the
theatre.

ALISON

The little place over there? It's a 50 seater!

MARY

But live.

ALISON

In Birmingham?

JACK

What's wrong with Birmingham?

ALISON

Nothing, nothing at all.

JACK

Good place.

ALISON

Absolutely. *(To MARY.)* Did Martin tell you I was with
Arts Ahoy? BBC 1 – top slot Fridays?

JACK

That's it! I seen you! I knew I clocked your boat!
You're with that programme! Hang on … hang on …
you're the one with the gear! Listen mate, compared
to you – Anthea Turner – crowshit!

ALISON

Oh, you are sweet.

JACK

Arlene – Anna – Alison! You're Alison Witherspoon! I
know your face better than me own Mum's.

ALISON

Come on, I'm just a presenter.

JACK

That's what I want to be. That's my dream!

ALISON

It's harder than it looks, Jack. Mary, I was
wondering … I'd love to interview you. Possibly a
whole programme. Just you, and … *(She gestures at
CYST.)*

MARY

We're hardly mainstream.

MARTIN

(*From the café.*) Ready!

ALISON rises.

ALISON

Oh, but you are! You could be. Do think about it.

She goes.

CYST

'Do think about it!'

JACK

Alison Witherspoon – she's fucking famous!

He goes inside.

MURIEL enters with a trug, crosses.

MURIEL

(*Pauses, then,*) Mary?

MARY

Mmm?

MURIEL

You won't let them put me in a home?

MARY

What?

MURIEL

I'd rather have my neck wrung when the time comes.

MARY

I'll see to it for you. (*Returns to his newspaper.*)

MURIEL smiles happily, goes.

CYST

Why doesn't she use the henna?

MARY

She says it's passé.

Pause as, heads down, they read the Sunday papers.

CYST suddenly gasps, throws his supplement away.

CYST

We're going to run out!

MARY

Run out of what?

CYST

(Ratty.) People! All these women not wanting fat
stomachs, and men getting sterile ... it's all going
to be done by robots. Chips servicing chips, a totally
silent world because there'll be no mouths left
to speak, ears left to hear, just radio waves in a
soundless, sightless ...

MARY

Shut up. The world's never going to run out of things
for you to worry about.

CYST

But Mary ...

MARY

That cyst on your neck is benign, for Christ's sake!!

CYST

They could have mixed up the plates. The biopsy
could have been entered on the wrong ...

MARY

Only on Channel 5! Listen, if it weren't benign, you'd
have been dead long ago. You are not, repeat not

going to be left, all on your own, the last basket-case
survivor on this planet.

CYST

You said yourself – we're all turning into functions ...

MARY

I was upset about the cat – and spare me your vulgar
sociology.

CYST

(*Head in the newspaper again.*) You said you
preferred it vulgar.

Giggles and moans from above from MARTIN and ALISON. MARY
stirs restlessly. The sounds build to a prolonged and vocal climax.

Silence.

CYST

Mary?

MARY buries himself in his newspaper.

CYST

You wanna fool around?

No response from MARY. CYST walks about.

CYST

You could be Prince Myshkin and I'll be the Snow
Queen.

No response from MARY.

CYST

What I'd really like is a quest.

He looks to MARY. Still no response.

> CYST

I'd be in this forest ... pitch black. Suddenly a shaft of light and a young fawn leaps across me path. I follow the light and then I see him. *(MARY'S attention is caught.)* Tall ... shining ... Rodolfo. With long white thighs like a pencil.

MARY considers this but goes back to his paper.

> CYST

What would you like? Young girls, I suppose.

> MARY

I'm not that insecure. *(He rises, exits.)*

> CYST

Where are you going?

The MUSIC of Jimmy Yancey's 'At the Window.'

Pause. MARTIN enters, smiles at CYST, throws himself down on the seat. Slight pause.

ALISON enters. She crosses, exits. MARTIN rises and follows her.

MARY enters, watches them go, turns back and exits.

CYST, seeing MARY watch the girl, gets up, grabs the papers and follows MARY inside.

MUSIC of 'At the Window' by Jimmy Yancey continues.

> *Fade to black and up again.*

JACK is fishing the pond. MARTIN lies stretched out, asleep, nearby. JACK fishes, for as long as it will hold, to the sound of 'At the Window.'

JACK shakes his head, puts down the fishing rod, goes inside.

MARTIN asleep. Small pause.

MURIEL enters, in a Red Riding Hood cloak, with a plate of cakes. She passes, then notices MARTIN, and approaches him.

He wakes with a start.

MURIEL

Macaroon?

He takes one.

MURIEL

Take two, take two.

She proffers the plate again, and again, until he has four macaroons. Placated, she smiles and goes inside. He bites into a large macaroon.

Light change.

ACT ONE - SCENE THREE

ALISON, MARY, in a Russian smock, JACK, CYST, in soft grey and brown tulle, and MARTIN, emerge severally. MARY with cigar and brandy, CYST with a very large, brightly painted cup of coffee, the others with their drinks.

ALISON

Sorry about your cat. I've got a gorgeous little Yorkie. Martin adores him.

They sit, relaxed after a good meal.

MARY

Do you?

MARTIN

Hate it.

CYST

(*Wistfully.*) I'd like a little dog.

MARY

What for?

CYST

Company.

MARY

You've got company.

JACK

You have to take him out, Cyst.

CYST

Why?

JACK

Exercise. Do his business.

MARY

Good. Get your weight down.

CYST

(*Puzzled.*) I'm not fat.

MARY

Nice little Yorkie yapping round your legs – you'd meet people ...

CYST

I don't wish to meet people.

MARY

(*To ALISON.*) See what I mean!

CYST

(*Embarrassed by ALISON'S presence.*) Will you shut up?

CYST turns away, upset.

> MARY
>
> Cyst, I am trying to help. Do you seriously intend to spend the rest of your days measuring out coke spoons at the back of a Handsworth garage? I mean – is this IT? Our existence to be a pastiche shrine to your paralyzing fearophobia? What games are we playing? I'm talking about my life here.

> CYST
>
> (*Hurt.*) Don't.

> JACK
>
> Cyst's always been shy, Mary.

> MARY
>
> Jack, we're all shy!

> ALISON
>
> I'm appallingly shy.

> MARY
>
> There you are! A woman who has the courage to admit it. And still speak to an audience of five million a week.

> ALISON
>
> Seven actually.

> MARY
>
> Seven. A woman who does things.

CYST moves away.

> MARY
>
> How long since you've been off this forecourt? You can't keep asking Muriel to shop for your personals.

CYST

She likes shopping.

MARY

That is not the point. It's you I'm worried about.
Perhaps you <u>should</u> get a dog – you could go down the
pub together.

CYST

I don't want to go down to the pub. Why should I
go down to the pub when we've evolved a perfectly
rational infra-structure here.

MARY

You've been talking to Herbie again.

CYST

What's wrong with that? Mary, don't be cheap! I've
re-planned my whole psychic structure on that talk
you had with Herbie after the wine-fest.

MARY

Just shut up.

CYST

I will not.

JACK

Oh, come on you two . . .

CYST

(*Together.*) Keep out of this, Jack.

MARY

(*Together.*) Stay out of it.

JACK

Okay. Don't bite me head off!

MARY

(*To JACK.*) You're so reasonable, of course. Your relationships are so urbane.

CYST

Sauve . . .

MARY

What?

CYST

(*Falters.*) Sauve?

MARY

Sauve? Sauve? Suave – you illiterate berk. 'Sauve!'

Furious at the faux-pas in front of ALISON, he dashes CYST'S cup to the ground and exits.

CYST

Oh, not the Clarice Cliff! He's ruined the set!

ALISON and MARTIN move away to the pool.

CYST

One of these days I'll surprise him.

JACK

Yeah, piss off.

CYST

Oh, I will, I will.

JACK

You're too meek.

CYST

(*Meekly.*) I know.

JACK

He'd be right choked if you walked out and got a job.

CYST

Where would I get a job?

JACK

Courier – on the package tours, you'd make a fortune.
Guy I know got the pie and mash concession for the
whole Costa – two seasons flat.

CYST

(*Slight pause.*) I do think about it. Sitting on one of
those tall stools ... low lights ... barman polishing
his glasses. I hear the bead curtains behind me ...
ticlung ... ticlung ... "Hello there." "Hullo." "What are
you drinking?" "Bacardi, if you insist." And, in the
corner, a little feller on the keyboards ...

JACK

There you go.

CYST

I'd not have the nerve. Anyway, what about my
appointments at the behaviour clinic?

JACK

You only went once.

CYST

(*Shrugs, then.*) I couldn't leave Mary.

JACK

He'd be laughing without you, mate. Doctors' bills,
chemists' bills, all those cyst investigations, before
that the bone marrow thing.

CYST

My spine kept itching. I couldn't leave him, break his
heart. And I hope you heard that. (*to MARY, at the
door.*) You've ruined the set.

MARY

(*Genial.*) Never apologize, never complain, never explain ... mark of the aristo. (*He embraces CYST.*) You're looking beautiful.

JACK

So, he should after that facial. (*CYST looks alarmed.*)

MARY

(*Cuddles CYST affectionately.*) What facial?

ALISON and MARTIN approach.

CYST

(*Nervous.*) It was wonderful, Mary. She uses essential oils ... no lanolin, that's sheep's grease, grows hair on your face, that's what Jacinth says. It takes three tons of geranium petals to make one drop of oil. Well, you can't expect it to be cheap.

MARY

How much did it cost?

CYST

Well, there was the dusting powder, the face dew, and moisturizer ... it all came in a set, special offer.

MARY

How much?

CYST

(*Slight pause.*) Ninety-eight pounds. (*Pause.*)

MARY

You spent ninety-eight quid on your face?

CYST

Yes ... feel. (*He lifts up his face, gets punched, falls.*) Ohh ... what did you do that for?

MARY

The world starves and this prick spends a hundred
quid on his face!

He makes to hit CYST again. MARTIN intervenes and holds onto
him, in a scuffle.

MARTIN

That's enough, Mary. Mary … that's enough!

MARY

(Pulls himself clear, exits, smashing things off the
table.) More than bloody enough.

CYST

(Wincing.) I knew it was too much at the time.

JACK

Well, don't feel too bad. He's just undone all the good
work.

ALISON

Are you all right?

CYST

(Ignores her.) I ought to have asked the price first,
but I didn't have the nerve. And I paid for Muriel.

JACK

Forget it. Look, point is, you gotta learn to stand up
for yourself …

They go.

MUSIC of Jimmy Yancey's 'How Long Blues' – up, and then down
under the next section.

ALISON

Well, well, well.

MARTIN

D'you want to split?

ALISON

I wonder if I should change channels.

MARTIN

You're doing okay.

ALISON

Okay is not where it's at.

MUSIC fades out.

ALISON

Why didn't you tell me?

MARTIN

What?

ALISON

About all these amazing weirdos! (*MARTIN does not reply.*) Why does he call himself Aunt Mary?

MARTIN

For tax purposes.

ALISON

(*Puzzled.*) Oh. Where does Jack feature?

MARTIN

(*Unwilling.*) Mary met him in rehab. Look, forget it.

ALISON

Are you kidding? They're a gift! There's a wonderful programme in this.

MARTIN

Time to go.

ALISON

(Shakes her head.) Uchuch.

MARTIN

Alison!

ALISON

It's perfect, the more I think about it. If all we
can afford is talking heads, let's have them
extraordinaire!

MARTIN

And you think they'll agree?

ALISON

They all agree. Wait till I lay this on Adrian, he'll shit
himself.

MARTIN

It's good you've smashing tits, love.

ALISON

Okay, Martin. You're a great pull. And you've had five
spots on the box, and I'm not talking panel games –
quality media exposure. Don't cock this up. If I can
just get a crew together!

MARTIN

Alison, they've got their own life here.

ALISON

Are you kidding? They'll be celebrities! My God . . .
a butch agony queen . . . fantastic talking point!
The fey one can have a spot to himself . . . clothes,
beauty hints I've got it! Their own chat show! *(He
groans.)* What's the matter? What are you doing? *(He
embraces her.)*

MARTIN

Your eyes are the colour of a Prussian cavalry
officer's greatcoat. Neither green nor blue, neither
blue nor green ...

ALISON

Don't change the subject.

MARTIN

And did I ever tell you about your arse? I must
have done. I think about it all the time. You ... are
Aphrodite.

ALISON

From Addlestone?

MARTIN

No. You were left in a basket in the reeds by the river
Wey. Your Mum came down to the water's edge to
wash the Tupperware ... and there you were ... the
face of a lily with purple-green eyes looking up at her.
What could she do? ... put your hand on me, come
on ... she stuffed you into her womb, like this ...
crawled back up the bank with you, one hand on you,
the other in the dirt ... "Look what I've got here!" ...
bet it gave your Dad a thrill ... do you like that?

ALISON

Oh ... you ... *(He kisses her.)* You think because you
turn me on ... *(He kisses her.)*

MARTIN

Don't do it.

ALISON

What have I got to lose?

MARTIN

Me?

They look at each other.

> Light change.

ACT ONE – SCENE FOUR

MURIEL'S BIRTHDAY PARTY.

CYST enters from within, wearing a half-made dress. MARY follows, tape measure round neck. CYST stands on chair, MARY pins the hem of the dress.

CYST

Why should I if I don't want to?

MARY

She's a guest, for Christ's sake. (*He pins.*) Okay, I made a pass. I was out of it on Muriel's sloe gin.

CYST

It's not just that. Every time she walks past, you ...

MARY

What?

CYST

Mary, if I was crude I'd say your dick hits your chin, but I'm not.

MARY

She's a pretty girl. (*He pins.*) Not beautiful, like you.

CYST

(Slightly mollified.) You know how I feel about casual sex.

MARY

(Sing-song.) Richard Gere ... Richard Gere!

CYST

And don't you love to spoil it with your mean horrible coarseness.

MARY

(Pinning.) If I'm coarse it's because you're such a wilting lily. Turn round. Did it never occur to you that the way you let me exploit you damages me? *(CYST turns to look at him, baffled.)* Have you asked Muriel about the jacket? *(CYST shakes his head.)* Why not?

CYST shrugs.

MARY

I see. I'm going to all this trouble and you're coming as Jane Eyre.

CYST

(Gets down.) That's it!

MARY

I haven't finished.

CYST

Shut up!

MARY

What's the matter?

CYST

Shut up! Shut up! Shut up!

MARY

We-ell! Now that is better.

CYST

No, it's not. Can't you understand? I don't want to
assert myself!

MARY

I see. And how else are you to make your way in the
world?

CYST

I don't want to make my way in the world.

MARY

Turn round.

CYST

Anyway, I hate parties. I never know what to say.

MARY

Just concentrate on looking beautiful.

CYST

Then they'll all look at me.

MARY

I'll tell them not to.

CYST

After all this trouble? Anyway, I'll know you told
them not to, and they'll know . . .

MARY

Okay.

CYST

. . . and I'll know they know . . .

MARY

Okay, Okay . . .

CYST

. . . and they'll know I know they know, and . . .

MARY

Okay, okay, stop! Breathe! In . . . out . . . in . . . out . . .
remember your yoga . . . imagine little gills in your
back . . . open them up . . . fill them out . . . in . . . that's
better. Stay with the breathing, I'll talk you through.
Here you are, approaching the door . . . pause . . .
breathe . . . you turn the knob . . . another breath . . .
don't hurry, lift your head . . . a quick look in the
glass . . . open the door, and glide through. (CYST
mimes.) Turn casually . . . take your time . . . take
your time . . . and drift slowly to the nearest person . . .
never mind who, don't start arguing with yourself –
just do it.

CYST

Suppose they're talking to someone?

MARY

Doesn't matter. Nobody minds. Nobody's saying
anything . . . come on . . .

CYST

(Deep breath.) Hullo, how are you, are you feeling all
right?

MARY

Fine, thanks, sweetie.

CYST

Oh good, take my time don't forget to smile . . . is it
Thursday, I thought it was Friday. I shall think it's

November next. Hang on, what was I saying? I've lost
the flow. Mary, I'm losing the flow . . .

MARY

I'll be Lady Rosemary, give you the idea. (*Perfect
upper class voice.*) Hellew! How was Saint Moritz?

CYST

Wet – I mean, snowy.

MARY

And the ball, the hunt ball?

CYST

Ah . . . . . .

MARY

Weren't you there? No, of course, you were in
Grimsby. Having a facial. Your turn.

CYST

What nice teeth, are they capped? I'd like mine done
but it costs unless you screw with the dentist. Is
yours Australian?

He reacts to MARY'S exaggerated Lady Rosemary stance.

MARY

What's the matter now? I'm trying to help.

CYST

No, you're not.

MARY

Then what am I doing here?

CYST

Trying to undermine me. As usual.

MARY

Rubbish! Look Cyst, anything I tell you is an act of
friendship. I care. Remember your crabs?

CYST

And who gave them to me?

MARY

I'm trying to help. Make you look – feel – lovely.
So that you won't let me down.

CYST

Let you down?

MARY

Babes, I want you to sparkle.

CYST

I have no intention of sparkling. And don't look so
dégagé, Mary. We all know what you'll be after.

MARY

Me?

CYST

May I remind you that it's Muriel's birthday, and I
will not have you degrade it with your full-frontal
fatuity.

MARY

Uh?

CYST

You never take your eyes off her.

MARY

Okay – pretty girl – she can sit on my face any time.
It doesn't affect us, it's what H.G. Wells called a
passade – a mood of the moment. Things will be all

the better between us. Let's face it, the earth shifted but infinitesimally this morning – still, you enjoyed yourself.

> CYST

I'm not coming.

> MARY

I'll be there for you.

> CYST

No, you won't.

> MARY

By your side, babes, like superglue.

> CYST

The whole evening?

> MARY

Never leave your side. I'll be waiting with a white orchid as you step through that door.

> CYST

And you won't desert me?

> MARY

As if.

He ushers CYST inside.

> MARY

(*As they go.*) What are you going to give us? Amanda and Eliot? Brief Encounter? What about your Blanche?

> *Light change.*

JACK in dark suit like a gangster, except for the trainers, brings out Japanese lanterns on poles. He and MARTIN, in a clean T-shirt, place them.

ALISON, in a gold scrap of a dress, emerges with hand lanterns. JACK and MARTIN bring, from around the up left corner of the house, a bare tree in a pot, festooned with cobwebs and deep red roses. JACK goes inside. ALISON laughs.

MARTIN

What?

ALISON

They're all so weird!

MARTIN

They're friends of mine.

ALISON

Who I'm trying to help!

MARTIN

Leave it.

ALISON

No. (*He cuddles her.*) Don't. You're getting to me.

MARTIN

Good.

ALISON

And wouldn't that just suit you? All mod-cons, three meals a day . . . 'Hush, kiddies, Daddy's writing.' Till my arse drops and some slightly-younger poetry-fest groupie sticks her boobs under your nose.

MARTIN

I'm just saying it's not for them. And lay off Mary.
There'll be trouble. Listen, why don't we walk in the
woods – watch the moon come up ...

ALISON

You mean you want a shag?

MARTIN

I want to look at the moon.

ALISON

(*Mock shock.*) Don't tell me you don't fancy it?

MARTIN

That depends. If there's a mossy bank where the wild
thyme blows ...

ALISON

We can do it here if you want.

MARTIN

... where oxlips and the nodding violet grows ...

ALISON

Is that what you want? Yes? No? Why are you looking
at me like that?

MARTIN

Like what?

ALISON

As though you'd stepped in a turd. I'm Aphrodite,
remember?

MARTIN

You're spitting in my face.

ALISON

Martin ... come on ... it's a leg-over! Do you want to go upstairs or not?

She stamps off inside. He hangs about, gazes up looking for the moon, then follows her inside.

The MUSIC of Jimmy Yancey's 'Jimmy's Stuff.'

MARY enters, elegant in a navy, unstructured suit. He escorts MURIEL, in a tea-gown, with embroidered bag and shoes with louis-heels.

JACK and ALISON follow. JACK pours a drink for MURIEL.

MURIEL

Ooh – when!

JACK gives her the hefty drink.

JACK

Mud in your eye, Mu!

The music switches to a tango.

MARY leads MURIEL in a decorously correct tango. Applause.

Musical cross to 'Jimmy's Stuff.'

MARY and ALISON begin to flirt, laughing.

CYST appears at the door in his new aubergine moiré dress, now with a silver, square-shouldered jacket over. He wears a small hat with veiling and a diamanté brooch, high heels and carries a clutch bag. He pauses in the doorway, is about to make his entrance, when JACK blunders inside for more beer, nearly knocking him over.

CYST hovers in the doorway, uncertain. As he makes to move again, JACK slops out with his refilled glass, so that they are jammed in the door. JACK spills beer on CYST'S skirt.

MUSIC switch to Jimmy Yancey's 'The Fives.'

ALISON and MARY, standing close together, laugh loudly.

MARTIN talks to MURIEL. JACK dances frenetically, and bumps into CYST as CYST approaches nervously.

CYST

Hullo how are you, do you like my gloves? I wanted plain but they only had these little daisy shapes. I picked out the stitching but the holes are still there. I keep pulling at them . . .

JACK

Keep on trucking, Cyst!

He dances away. MARTIN crosses for a drink.

The MUSIC changes to 'How Long Blues.'

MARY and ALISON begin to dance, going at once into a clinch.

CYST walks stiffly to the drinks table, but just misses MARTIN, who moves away just as he approaches.

CYST stands, too rigid to help himself to a drink. He picks up a half-filled glass left by someone else, holds it rigidly – propped up against the table.

Lights crossfade.

JACK lies at MURIEL'S feet. ALISON sits on MARY'S knee, arms about him, listening to MARTIN reading a poem. He too is at MURIEL'S feet, like Dejeuner sur L'herbe.

MUSIC CONCRETE, low.

MARTIN

In the crystal of the cave,
Temper iron, conquer steel,
Lest bicuspids both anneal,

Hissing, Arthur's living stave.
Clear the air with bitter smoke,
And to marinate the word,
Foil the tongue in buttered curd,
Wrapped in a sweet almond cloak.
Break the flint, reveal the core,
Rocketry beneath the shine,
Detonators crystalline,
Venomed eyeteeth in the maw.
Open sesame, says the boy,
Abra, Cadabra, and breaks the toy.

MURIEL

Thank you, Martin.

JACK

What's it called?

MARTIN

Geode.

JACK

Oh. Right.

MARY

(Slight pause.) Cyst! Your turn.

CYST panics. He looks to MARY for help. MARY'S gaze is cool. This
hardens CYST. He comes forward, in character.

CYST

'I don't want realism ... I want magic.'

MARY

Oh, not bloody Blanche again!

MURIEL

(Murmurs) Mary ...

MARY

I'm up to here with bloody Blanche.

MARTIN

Don't be such a prick.

ALISON

I haven't heard it.

MARY

The night is yet young.

MURIEL

But not for me, my dears. I must be off. My thanks
to you. Again. My word, I shall have a lot to tell God
tonight.

JACK puts her cloak about her shoulders.

MARTIN

He knows already, doesn't He?

MURIEL

Then He's going to hear it all again. Goodnight
everyone. God bless. And thank you for my lovely
birthday ... my nicest ever. (*As JACK relieves her of
her presents and escorts her off.*) Oh, thank you dear.

MARY clasps ALISON closer. They dance.

ALISON

We'd better be careful.

MARY

Why, babe?

ALISON

I don't want to upset Cyst.

MARY

What do you mean? What are you talking about?

ALISON

I thought you two were an item.

MARY

Me and Cyst? Just good friends.

ALISON

(Calls to CYST.) I adore your frock.

MARY

Having a good time, lover?

CYST strikes at ALISON with a knife. ALISON screams and slips.

MARTIN

What's up? What's the matter?

MARY

You okay, babes?

MARTIN

It's all right ... you're all right, love ... it's all right.
You're okay. *(He and MARY take ALISON inside.)*

CYST walks slowly to the pond. He throws down the knife, picks up two heavy stones, puts them in the pockets of his jacket, and walks into the pond.

The lights begin to fade. A spot picks up Cyst's scarf, caught in the tree overhanging the pond.

Fade to black.

ACT TWO

<u>ACT TWO – SCENE ONE</u>

The set is the same.

The party decorations have been cleared. MARTIN and JACK stand by the pond.

JACK

Smartie? *(JACK gives MARTIN a Smartie.)*

MARTIN

Thanks.

A FROGMAN emerges from the pond.

JACK

Anything?

The FROGMAN shakes his head, and goes inside. MARTIN and JACK contemplate the pond.

JACK

Quite a few finds today. Music centre, motor bike, revolver ...

MARTIN

(No reaction.) Nothing else?

JACK

Nah. This is going to mess up next season's theatre.

MARTIN

How do you mean?

JACK

Cyst was down for the old serpent of the Nile.

MARTIN

Cyst? Cleopatra?

JACK

You should have seen his Hedda Gabler, mate. Take
the roof off your mouth.

JACK tips more Smarties into MARTIN'S hand.

JACK

What happened to your bird?

MARTIN

Split.

They eat their Smarties.

JACK

Poor old Cyst.

MARTIN

Yeah. (*He sighs, reminiscent.*) I was taken for gay
once. Down the fifties shop. The girl there said I
looked like James Dean.

JACK

(*Disbelieving.*) What was you wearing?

MARTIN

Drainpipes, striped socks, fluorescent T-shirt. My
body looked really good.

JACK

Yeah?

MARTIN

The only trouble was it made my face look ugly. The
girl I was with nearly blurted it out, which would have
been great. I have this fantasy that the girl I live with

should be able to read my thoughts. Anyway, all she said was I had a self-conscious look on my face. Which was true.

JACK

What was her name?

MARTIN

Roberta. Amateur film maker. She was the one said I looked gay.

JACK

Yeah?

MURIEL enters, with a dark velvet cloth for the table.

MARTIN

All set?

MURIEL

Nearly ready. Look, I've finished my sampler.

JACK

(*Reads.*) 'We absolutely owe it to Our Lord never to be afraid of anything.'

MURIEL

I made it for poor Cyst.

She takes the sampler, and goes into the house.

MARTIN

Think they'll come up with anything? I don't know. Bloody mystery. Where's he gone?

JACK

Listen mate. Cyst would never walk off this forecourt. He's in there. (*Jerks his head towards pond.*)

                    MARTIN
They haven't found him.

                    JACK
Not into time and a half yet, are they?

MARTIN moves apart. A MAN arrives with a petrol can.

                    JACK
Run out, mate?

                    MAN
Yeah.

JACK fills the can, and takes the money.

                    MAN
Thanks. (*He goes.*)

MARTIN crosses, switches off forecourt lights.

                    JACK
Ready?

                    MARTIN
Yeah.

They go off.

MUSIC.

Procession enters. MURIEL first in a long dress of panne velvet, with an Edith Sitwell head-dress. She carries a large crystal ball, which she places on the table.

JACK carries a goblet and a stuffed owl. MARTIN carries candles, and lastly MARY, who looks menacing in a black suit and Homburg hat.

The procession moves formally round the forecourt, to the strains of *Schubert's B Flat posthumous piano sonata*, and then around the table. MARY removes his hat.

                    MURIEL

(Quietly.) His favourite piece.

She lifts the goblet, from which they drink in turn.

                    MURIEL

To Cyst ... beloved Cyst.

                    MARTIN

To Cyst, wherever you are.

                    JACK

You were a good mate, Cyst.

MARY takes the goblet and drinks needfully. MURIEL rescues it.
The MUSIC ends. Silence.

                    MURIEL

Will you all be seated please?

They sit around the table.

                    MURIEL

Is everyone ready? Touch hands, please.

                    JACK

Like this?

                    MURIEL

That's it. Mary?

MARY puts his hands on the table.

                    MURIEL

(Quavery voice.) Is there anybody there? *(Pause.)*
Is anybody there?

Pause. Then JACK scrapes his chair.

MURIEL

Keep still, Jack, there's a dear. We'll try again. Is
anybody there? Speak up. Is anybody there?

A whoo-whoo, which makes everyone jump.

JACK

Shit!

MARTIN

What was that?

MURIEL

Is there anybody there?

VOICE

(*Faint.*) Yes . . . .

MURIEL

Who is it? Who are you? Don't be shy . . .

VOICE

It's me-eee . . . . . .

MURIEL

Is that you, dear?

VOICE

Ye-es! Is that you?

MURIEL

Yes, it's me. How are you?

CYST

All right, how are you?

MURIEL

I'm very well . . .

MARY

Muriel, if we could get on please . . .

MURIEL

Of course. What did you want to say, Cyst dear?

JACK

Cyst?

MARTIN

Cyst?!

MURIEL

We're all listening.

CYST

Is Mary on his knees?

MURIEL

(Whispers to MARY.) He wants you on your knees,
Mary.

MARY gets on his knees.

MURIEL

We're ready. Hullo, are you there?

CYST

I'm here.

MURIEL

Go on dear. Give us your message.

CYST

Mary should say after me … 'I was unfair to Cyst.'

MARY

I was unfair to Cyst.

CYST

'Brutal' …

MARY

Brutal.

                    CYST

'Insensitive' . . .

                    MARY

Insensitive.

                    CYST

'Dogmatic' . . .

                    MARY

Dogmatic.

                    CYST

'Exploitative' . . .

                    MARY

Exploitative.

                    CYST

'Mean' . . .

                    MARY

Mean?

                    CYST

'Mean.'

                    MARY

Mean.

                    CYST

'And an indifferent and uninventive lover'.

                    MARY

What? Oh, all right.

                    CYST

Say it.

MARY

An indifferent and uninventive lover. You don't have
to show me up. Is that all? Cyst?

CYST

I forgive you. I forgive you for being a lush, an
opportunist and a loud-mouthed bully.

MARY

I know, baby, I know. It's true, I know, I know.

CYST

Stay on your knees. Repent.

MARY

Oh, I do, I do. I'm lost without you, lover. My life's gone
all dry, like wire. Cyst ... take me with you. Don't
leave me. Let me come with you. Let me in, Cyst. Let
me in ... Please ...

Weird sound and bright light.

CYST is standing in the doorway in a suit, wearing a hat. ALISON is
standing behind him. They enter ... and burst out laughing.

CYST doffs his hat, and places it merrily on ALISON'S head.

MARTIN

Cyst?

JACK

Cyst!

MARTIN

Cyst!

MURIEL

No – not Cyst. Francis.

MARTIN & JACK

Francis?

CYST

That is my name. Please don't call me Cyst. I have no cyst. Or, to be accurate, I have a small cyst – which is benign.

He sits, and crosses a leg. MARY is sick in the pond.

JACK

Is it really you Cyst? I mean Brian ... ah ... Francis? I don't get it.

MURIEL

(To CYST.) Your goldfish died, dear. We had to put him down the lavvy.

CYST

Farewell Frederick!

ALISON

Is Mary all right?

MARY staggers to his feet, coughing.

MARY

You real?

CYST

Of course.

MARY

Where were you? I thought you were in that pond for Christ's sake!

CYST

I was. It was finally and overtly apparent to me that I meant nothing to you as you never lost an opportunity to humiliate me as publicly as possible. And since the only human relationship I had ever been able to sustain was with someone whom I now saw to be base, I concluded that I, too, as I had always suspected, was of no value whatsoever. I decided to follow Virginia's example.

MARY

Virginia Woolf? You hate all those cock-suckers! Anyway ... anyway ... how come if you drowned yourself, you're sitting here in a Tommy Hilfiger suit?

CYST

The water wasn't deep enough.

MARY

So?

CYST

It's a long story.

MARY

Don't make it too long.

MURIEL

Mary ...

MARY

Jesus Christ, I been out of my mind. I thought you were dead!

He cries.

MURIEL

Ohh! *(She gives him a handkerchief from CYST'S breast pocket.)*

MARY

Cyst…

CYST

Please call me Francis.

MARY

Francis? Your name's not Francis, it's fucking
Jeffrey.

CYST

I have been renamed.

MARY

Who by?

CYST

Myself. I have renamed myself. A new name to go
with my new self. I have been reborn.

ALISON claps.

MARY

All right Miss Mouth, so where do you figger in this?
(*He grabs ALISON.*) I've been having the pond
dragged for fuck's sake!

CYST

Mary, release that woman!

MARY, surprised, does so.

CYST

I took assertion therapy. The intensive course.

MARY

How much?

CYST

A thousand pounds. (*MARY groans.*) It was intensive.

MARY

You're not kidding! (*To ALISON.*) This your idea?

MARTIN

Leave it, Mary. He's back! And you started it, waving your weapon in my bird's face.

ALISON

Martin, I do not need you to do the big protection act.

MARTIN

Oh great.

MARY

Right, Sir fucking Lancelot. Watch it, baby, you're just the scoop of vanilla for Frau Culture-Vulture here . . .

ALISON

Whereas you are the aristocracy of chic. Tell me, what is supposed to be so thrilling about a set of shacks with a half-arsed chicken house theatre the size of a toilet?

She moves aside as MARTIN and JACK help MURIEL repack her basket.

ALISON

If you really are who you say you are, I could get you a Booker Prize in six months! I'm trying to do you a favour for God's sake!

Silence.

MARY

(*To CYST.*) What happened?

Silence.

ALISON

Francis came to my room to apologise. We talked, and
I drove him up to town.

Pause.

MARY

Well, well. Well, well, well.

MURIEL

(*Anxious.*) Mary, don't break the furniture.

MARY walks up and down. And then turns on CYST.

MARY

Who would have believed it? Fucking sea-green
incorruptible. All it takes is two seconds of sweet talk.
What happened to your head? I'm tired. I'm going to
bed.

He goes.

MARTIN

I think we should leave.

ALISON

We'll talk about it. (*They go inside.*)

Pause.

JACK

Nice night. Wonder if they're biting?

CYST

(*Gives MURIEL her basket.*) Oh, Muriel, you're
wearing your Erté cloak!

MURIEL

We were going to bury you in it.

CYST reacts with pleasure, then realises the import of this and blenches.

> MURIEL

All right, dear?

> CYST

(Sad.) No. It's starting to wear off. The course. They didn't tell you that.

> JACK

What are you going to do?

> CYST

I don't know, Jack.

> MURIEL

Why not sleep on it? *(She rises.)* But do remember, it doesn't matter who you're with. Just so long as it's someone. You don't have to like them all the time. *(She moves off, pauses.)* My mother could be very spiteful. I wasted so much time resenting her. *(Walks off.)* Now she's gone. *(Exits.)*

> JACK

Time for kip?

> CYST

I'll just watch the bats over the water.

> JACK

Okay, mate. Good to see you.

> CYST

Thanks, Jack. Goodnight.

JACK moves off, stops and turns.

JACK

Mary's been very rough, you know. (*Exits.*)

Pause. MARY enters.

MARY

We're out of tea and Seven-Up.

Pause.

CYST

About the money – for the course.

MARY

Forget it. Half of it's yours anyway.

Pause. CYST picks at the crease in his trousers.

CYST

It wasn't worth it. Just another nest of adders.

Pause.

MARY

I thought you were dead.

Pause.

CYST

Pretty hysterical thing to do.

MARY

No, you were right.

CYST

I am calmer. (*MARY pours himself a generous drink.*)
Don't. I'll only have to clean up after you.

MARY puts down the glass.

MARY

(*Short pause.*) Were you ... thinking of staying?

CYST

I don't know.

MARY

This is your home. *(CYST looks away.)* You don't get on
with strangers. *(Takes a drink.)*

CYST smooths his trouser leg absently.

CYST

Maybe I should try living alone.

MARY

You'd go funny. Don't turn me away, Cyst. *(Drinks.)*

CYST

You can't even call me by my right name!

MARY

Sorry. Jeffrey.

CYST

If you didn't drink so much!

MARY

Why not? Conscious, daily demolition . . . who
dreamed up that sweet notion? I crumble, therefore
I am.

CYST

Same for all of us.

MARY

Perhaps if you didn't hate yourself you could stand
getting old.

CYST

Don't. *(As MARY refills his glass and drinks.)* I might
as well leave.

MARY

No.

CYST

A woman has only to set foot on that forecourt ...

MARY

I don't want a woman!

CYST

Yes, you do.

MARY

That was a long time ago.

CYST

You called me by her name last week.

MARY

When?

CYST

In bed.

Pause.

MARY

Skin like a pearl. Hair like a roomful of gold from the Brothers' Grimm. Even the fluff under her arms was pale. I ruined peoples' lives for that woman.

CYST

Mary ...

MARY

Know what she really liked? Her idea of the life of the soul? Karaoke.

CYST

It was just sex, Mary.

MARY

Sex? You kidding? Every time we screwed she had
her head turned to the bloody video – oh Christ, I'm
going to be sick again.

CYST

Mind the irises.

MARY is sick again. CYST gets blue paper from the roll, and
sponges him down.

MARY

You shouldn't do that. You shouldn't have to clear up
after me.

CYST

It's better than leaving it to dry. Come on.

MARY groans.

MUSIC. 'At the Window' ... low.

CYST

You feeling bad?

MARY

It's this pain again. D'you think it's prostate?
I'm not old enough for that, am I?

CYST

It's the drink.

MARY

I don't even care for it. Damn bad for you. You going to
roll me something sweet?

CYST

(Helping him inside.) I'm going to roll you into your
bed.

Fade to black.

The MUSIC of 'At the Window.'

<u>ACT TWO – SCENE TWO</u>

MARTIN enters with a tray containing a bottle of champagne and two glasses. He is followed by JACK bearing a pink, white and gold painted hip bath, full of foam.

> JACK
>
> Where does he want this?

MARTIN points down centre.

MARY enters in a T-shirt and chinos. He bears a tray.

> MARY
>
> Finished?

> MARTIN
>
> Yuh.

> MARY
>
> OK. Thanks.

They go.

MARY tests the water in the bath with his elbow, pours in scent, and bath salts ... gives a piercing whistle.

> CYST
>
> (*Off.*) Coming. (*He enters in a beautiful robe.*)

> MARY
>
> You look like a summer morning.

CYST

Thank you. (*He gets into the bath, closes his eyes.*)
Oh, it's lovely!

MARY sprinkles him with rose petals.

MARY

June roses. What is it Vanya says? Autumn roses . . .
mournful autumn roses . . .

CYST

(*Correcting him lazily.*) Exquisite, mournful roses.

MARY

Then he takes to the gun.

CYST

He doesn't shoot anyone. He misses.

MARY

A certain amount of cheating on Chekhov's part.
Stand up.

CYST

I can't. How can I?

MARY

What's the matter?

CYST

I told you I didn't want to come out here!

MARY

So, who's looking? If they are, they're in for a treat.
Oh, see to yourself! I'm never allowed to enjoy . . .

He walks away.

CYST

Mary, I can't reach my duck.

MARY

Fuck your duck.

Slight pause.

CYST

You are silly.

MARY

If you say so.

CYST

Good. That's something we agree on. (*Plays with foam.*)

MARY

I could try to change. (*CYST gives him a look.*)
Do you think I could?

CYST

Don't ask me. Ask yourself.

MARY

No. Pretty hopeless. Me and you. The two of us.
Together.

CYST

Stop trailing your coat, Mary.

MARY crosses, gives CYST his duck. CYST plays with the duck.
MARY stands over him.

CYST

(*Looks up.*) Are you in a hurry?

MARY

No, no. Carry on. (*He walks away. CYST continues to
mess about. MARY approaches again . . . hovers.*)

CYST

Mary, what is it? Whatever it is, say it. You're
beginning to unnerve me.

MARY

I don't know how to say it. (*He moves away again.*)

CYST

What is it? What have you been up to?

MARY

Nothing.

CYST

Is it the bookmaker?

MARY

No!

CYST

You can tell me. (*Short pause.*) It can't be that
terrible. Can it? Oh Mary, what have you done?

MARY

(*Dashes to the side of the bath and kneels.*) Cyst, will
you do me the honour of marrying me? I promise to
love and cherish you for the rest of my life, and all
my worldly goods. Don't answer at once think about
it. Take as long as you like. If the answer's no, I'll
understand. I'm no catch, I know, and you could do
better for yourself – but I love you.

Silence. CYST rises slowly, puts out a hand.

CYST

Help me out, please.

MARY wraps him in a towel with discreet reverence.

MARY

Well?

CYST

Well what?

MARY

What's your answer?

CYST

I'll give it to you in the morning.

MARY

It's morning now.

CYST

Tomorrow morning.

MARY

Tomorrow morning? I can't wait that long!

CYST

(*Ratty.*) Oh, all right, yes.

They embrace. ALISON enters.

ALISON

Hullo, could I talk to you if it's not a bad moment. Is it
a bad moment?

MARY

Yes.

CYST

(*Together.*) Yes.

ALISON

Oh, sorry. It was just that Francis and I had such a
fruitful talk on the train coming up . . .

MARY

Congratulate me!

ALISON

Why?

MARY

I'm getting married.

ALISON

Oh? *(Swift look to CYST for his reaction.)* Who to?

CYST

Me.

ALISON

Sorry?

CYST

We're engaged.

MARY

Cyst has done me the honour of accepting my hand.
He's consented to be my wife.

ALISON

Oh. Oh? Oh! Ah. Well … congratulations … my very
best wishes to you both. Am I the first to know?
Marvellous … fantastic … this is great. Are you
kidding?

MARY

No.

ALISON

No. Right. Smashing … no, stunning – no, I mean it.
(She embraces them.)

CYST

Thank you.

ALISON

I can see that it's probably not the moment to bring
up the programme. On the other hand, given your
news . . . Mary, I don't know if Francis mentioned it,
but I saw my people when I was in town and they're
definitely interested in building a show around you.
It's too early to talk further than a pilot, but Marcus –
that's my Controller – is very hot, so it would be a
question of moving fairly swiftly into format, if that's
okay. Actually, if you've got a mo, I did a few roughs.
I mean, you're welcome to bring things of your own,
but you'll find it helpful to fall back on our experience.
We have our uses.

MARY

You do, you do.

ALISON

Why don't I fetch them down? (*Turns at the door.*)
The bread situation could be fairly intriguing. In
terms of network, residuals, spin-off, cable, foreign
rights . . . you name it! See you! (*She goes.*)

MARY turns, gives CYST a champagne glass, opens the champagne
and pours.

CYST

You had it ready!

MARY

To you.

CYST

(*They drink.*) You must have been pretty sure of me.

MARY

I just wanted the scenario to be right if you said yes.
To my bride.

CYST

Ooh! Straight up my nose.

MARY

Come on.

CYST

(*Follows, then stops short.*) Oh . . .

MARY

What is it?

CYST

The ring. My engagement ring. Where's my ring?

MARY

Nearly forgot. (*He pushes a ring on CYST'S finger.*)

CYST

Oh, Mary! (*Embracing MARY, he regards his own
hand draped around MARY'S neck.*) Just a minute.

MARY

What's the matter? What's up?

CYST

I know this ring. It's Muriel's fiancé's signet ring.

MARY

She wants you to have it.

CYST

(*Looks down at the ring, then.*) Oh, all right.

He goes, followed by MARY.

Pause.

ALISON enters, and looks about.

ALISON
Damn. (*Goes inside again.*)

Light change.

ACT TWO – SCENE THREE

Bright sunshine.

MARTIN and JACK enter, dressed up for the wedding. JACK carries a huge, beautiful arrangement of white lilies.

JACK
Fell off the back of a hearse. Not a word to Cyst.
Don't want another funeral.

MURIEL enters, wheeling a huge, tiered cake on a trolley.

MURIEL
You don't think I've gone too far?

MARTIN
Fantastic. Pure Ludwig of Bavaria.

JACK
Cyst'll love it.

MURIEL, happy, wheels the cake inside.

MARTIN and JACK bring out the seating for the wedding, and a small dais. They sit down, with cans of beer.

JACK
How was the gig in Weymouth? Make anything?

MARTIN

Nah – free Festival. Just, you know – (*JACK looks baffled*) bit of body-painting – existential juggling –

JACK

What's that?

MARTIN

No balls.

Silence.

MARTIN

Alison thinks I'm nuts.

JACK

Yeah?

MARTIN

Says I'm a romantic. Reckons I'd get a real rucking from her women friends. Which is odd since the ones she's introduced me to have all tried to go to bed with me.

JACK

Ah, knock it on the head.

MARTIN

(*Reverently.*) You've seen her arse, Jack.

They jump as ALISON, dressed for the wedding, appears with decorations. They are in the way, so they go inside.

ALISON arranges the decorations as MURIEL wanders by with a trug of flowers. ALISON cuts her off.

ALISON

Stunning flowers.

MURIEL smiles, moves away. ALISON pursues her.

ALISON

Muriel, do you know them well?

MURIEL

Of course! I grew them all myself.

ALISON

I meant Mary and Francis.

MURIEL tries to move off.

ALISON

How long have you known them?

MARY comes out in a white towelling bath-robe.

MARY

Mu?

ALISON, seeing she is not wanted, goes inside.

MARY

Do you think I'm doing the right thing here? Tying
myself down?

MURIEL

My dear. *(They walk.)* All I know is – it's usually
better than the alternative.

MARY stops. MURIEL stands on tiptoe, kisses him on the cheek.
They stand, holding hands.

MARY

Thanks, Muriel. I got a fit of the wobbles there.

MURIEL

Everyone does.

She looks up at him smiling.

                    MARY
Thanks for everything.

He bends to kiss her hand. She jerks it away abruptly.

                    MARY
What is it, doll? What's the matter?

                    MURIEL
It isn't correct, Mary. Only married women get their
hands kissed. I'm not married.

She goes inside. MARY is nonplussed. Then follows her inside.

Jimmy Yancey MUSIC plays, which becomes sumptuous Handel.

ALISON and MURIEL appear and take their seats. The opening of
'Here Comes the Bride' – quickly aborted.

MARY comes out, elegant in an Armani suit and satin tie. He is
very nervous. ALISON rises and sets him in the right spot before
the small dais.

They wait.

And wait.

There is a sudden very loud burst of MUSIC – Zadok the Priest.

MARTIN and JACK appear and pick up leafy branches from each
side of the door, holding them to make an arch.

CYST appears in the doorway. He wears a pale cream wedding
dress, low-waisted, trimmed with lace and satin, head-dress low on
the brow, straight narrow skirt with train à la Twenties. He carries
a sheaf of Easter lilies and steps forward, composed and grave, and
approaches MARY'S side.

ALISON, as bridesmaid, steps in behind him carrying a small
bouquet. CYST wavers. ALISON takes his bouquet.

MARTIN steps up on to the dais, carrying a prayer book.

> MARTIN
>
> Dearly beloved … we are gathered together here, in the sight of God, to join together this man, and this man, in holy matrimony …

MURIEL coughs and sniffs.

> MARTIN
>
> … which is an honourable estate, instituted by God in the times of man's innocency, and is not by any *(raises his voice as MURIEL begins to sob)* to be enterprised lightly or wantonly, but reverently and discreetly, advisedly and soberly. Muriel, what's the matter?

MURIEL is now sobbing uncontrollably.

> ALISON
>
> Carolle, are you all right?

> JACK
>
> Mu?

> CYST
>
> Hortense?

MURIEL accepts a large handkerchief, and tries to stop, shaking her head sadly.

> CYST
>
> Oh Hortense!

MARY cuddles MURIEL. The spasm comes to an end.

MURIEL

My dears, can you ever forgive me? Whatever
happened? What came over me? I'm so very sorry. To
interrupt at such a moment . . .

MARY

That's okay, babe.

CYST

You were always so wonderfully emotional, Hortense.

MURIEL

I'm a fool.

MARY

No, you're not.

MURIEL

You've been so good to me. When I retired from
nursing, I thought my life was over. Instead, when
you came, my life began.

MARY

You cured Cyst's warts, first week we were here.

MURIEL

Forgive me. I've not been myself these last few days.
I've been afraid it's all over.

MARY

What do you mean?

MURIEL

(With a quick glance at ALISON.) If you're away a lot.

CYST

We're not going away. This is our home.

JACK

I'm not going anywhere.

MURIEL

I'm so sorry. I've never really liked weddings – not
since my darling Ronald fell out of the sky. I miss him
so much. (*She puts a gloved hand on CYST'S arm.*)
Forgive me, Mary. It's just that I've never known
rapture. It leaves a gap.

Silence. CYST cuddles MURIEL, who looks very small.

MARY

(*Calls*) Marty.

They confer, apart. MARY beckons to CYST, and they confer.

CYST looks surprised, thinks, then nods soberly. MARY and CYST
stand, side by side – now facing downright, instead of up left.
MARTIN stands, facing them upstage.

MARY indicates for MURIEL to stand on his other side.

MARTIN

Dearly beloved ... I'll get straight to it. Do you, Aunt
Mary, take Francis – and Hortensia ...

MURIEL

(*As light dawns.*) Oh! (*She smiles up at AUNT MARY.*)

JACK swiftly takes the small bouquet from ALISON, and thrusts
it in MURIEL'S hands.

MARTIN

... to be your lawful wedded wives?

MARY

I do. And I do.

MARTIN

Do you, Hortensia and Francis – Muriel and Cyst –
take Aunt Mary to be your lawful wedded husband?

CYST

I do.

MURIEL

I do, too.

MARTIN

I now pronounce you man and wives. You may kiss
the brides.

MARY takes a turn, with his brides.

MARTIN throws confetti, MURIEL throws her posy to ALISON en
passant, and JACK and MARTIN make an archway for the bridal
exit.

The sound of bells.

Fade to black.

ACT TWO – SCENE FOUR

The setting as before.

Some of the wedding decorations are still in place. Glasses and
bottles about, and streamers … evidence of a party.

ALISON enters on her mobile.

ALISON

Jeremy? Alison. Have you got Adrian? … Well, where
is he? Never mind. If you see him tell him I'm at the
Handsworth number – and counting. He'll understand.

She dials again.

ALISON

Hullo ... good morning. Is Sir Marcus at home? ...
Alison Witherspoon ... Thank you so much ...
Marcus? Hullo! Sorry to break in on a Sunday
morn. I'm trying to raise the elusive Adrian ...
What? Marcus, that's very naughty. He is not a
big girl's blouse, well, only on weekends. I think
you're terribly crude. Crude and lovely. Look,
I just absolutely need your gut response on
this Handsworth project. I'm making fantastic
progress! ... Oh, they're playing hard to get, but we
all know that one. They're dying to get out of the
sticks and –

MARTIN enters, hungover.

ALISON

– hang on ... oh, it's only Martin. Marcus there is
one teeny thing. I mean, without going over anyone's
head, this is my show ... If I could just have your ...
Oh, that's marvellous of you. Sorry? ... Oh, but
I'd love to! That's an enchanting idea. That's very
special of you ... And to you. (*She makes a kissing
sound, replaces the receiver. To MARTIN:*) It's in the
bag!
(*Goes inside.*)

Slight pause. JACK enters, jaunty, till the light hits him.

JACK

Aw! Aw ... must have been all that head-banging.

MARTIN

(*In pain.*) No. Jack Daniels.

CYST enters, in a new negligée, with a very large box of chocolates. He is humming. He proffers chocolates. JACK and MARTIN shake their heads. CYST settles on the swing seat with a glossy magazine.

Short pause.

MARY staggers on in vest and pyjama bottoms and dark glasses. He groans.

CYST

(*Without looking up.*) Do you want some Andrews?

MARY groans.

CYST

You've only yourself to blame.

MARY

What was I on, for Christ's sake?

CYST

You started with the punch.

MARY

(*Groans.*) That was for the band . . .

CYST

. . . then sidecars with Muriel and myself, Carlsberg with the curry, champagne for the toasts – that fizzy red stuff . . .

MARY

All right, all right, no need to be so fucking unctuous.

CYST

Unctuous? I hadn't an unctuous thought in my head.

MARY mutters. CYST picks up a new magazine, reads.

JACK crosses, inspects his fishing line, re-baits and waits by the pool for a bite.

> CYST
>
> Oh no!

> MARY
>
> What?

> CYST
>
> Listen to this. 'By taking the' ... hold on, I've lost my place ... no, that's right ... I was there ... 'by taking the temperature of the sky ... '

> MARY
>
> The what?

> CYST
>
> The sky! (*Starts again, patiently.*) 'By taking the temperature of the sky, scientists have deduced that the Milky Way is moving at an unexpectedly high speed!'

> MARY
>
> So?

> CYST
>
> The sky ... at high speed! Ohh!

> MARY
>
> Look, buck up or shut up. I'm getting a serious surge to the head.

> CYST
>
> The Big-Bang theory! The Pope settled for Big-Bang twenty years ago 'cause it fits in with Genesis.

MARY

Stuff the Pope.

CYST

Mary! I may be lapsed, but I'm not having that.

MARY

Fuck off.

CYST

And stop saying fuck! You blur the meaning of a
transcendental experience, donated by God for our
delight and the procreation of . . .

MARY

All right, all right.

CYST

I don't think my stance over damn's unreasonable,
and I'll tolerate bollocks . . .

MARY

You've made your point.

CYST

. . . not bloody, which . . .

MARY

Cyst . . . !

CYST

. . . you know very well to be a contraction of By Our
Lady, thus to a Catholic, even a lapsed Catholic . . .
(MARY blows a gasket and shoves him on the floor.)
You are nothing but a cruel, vicious bully!

MARY

Arseholes.

                    CYST

Serve you right if I had drowned.

                    MARY

Bollocks.

MURIEL enters.

                    CYST

(Sweetly.) Morning, Hortense.

MARY buries his head in a magazine.

                    CYST

She heard that, didn't you, Hortense?

                    MURIEL

(Innocent.) What dear? Oh, thank you Mary. *(As
MARY arranges cushions for her.)*

                    MARY

One of my wives loves me.

                    CYST

Piss off.

ALISON enters.

                    ALISON

Good morning, good morning. Fantastic news. I've
just spoken to Adrian on the phone!

                    MARY

Oh yeah?

                    ALISON

They're over the moon! I didn't know you were cult
figures with the cognoscenti top brass. Martin, why
didn't you tell me?

MARTIN

(*In pain.*) What?

ALISON

It's looking good! Oh, by the way, who's your agent?

CYST

Agent?

ALISON

Don't you have an agent? A literary agent?

CYST

No.

ALISON

My God, you'll be flayed alive. You'll need someone
to handle your performance side. I'll ring Rodney. I
can't promise, but I'll twist his arm. Do you mind if I
take a few pics?

MURIEL

Oh, thank you dear. (*She sits up straight, pats her
hair.*)

ALISON takes pictures.

ALISON

This is great!

MARY

(*Cool.*) Yeah?

ALISON

I'm just getting a composite together. To give people
the feel of your set-up. (*She crosses, stands on a
stone, surveys the scene.*) Just think ... five years
from now you could have a thousand seater here,
with a restaurant complex. Another Glyndebourne,

without the draggy bits. Of course, all this will have to go. Is that big field yours? The one with the flowers?

JACK

Yeah.

ALISON

There you are. There's your car park. By the way, Adrian wants to come down and meet you.

She stands over MARY, who squints up at her.

MARY

You really do have great legs, baby.

ALISON

(*Smiles.*) Thanks. He's free on Thursday. What about Thursday?

MURIEL

Ooh, I forgot! I've brought the honeymoon brochures. I'm afraid Greece will be very hot.

CYST

Let's wait for winter ... go back to Jamaica. Oh, Hortense, wait till you see! Palm trees dipping ... pelicans skimming. Remember the picnic on the shore, Mary?

MARY

You bet.

CYST

Elgar's Shed music playing ...

MARY

Rack of lamb burning slow ... (*He gets up, stretches.*) I'm feeling better.

He helps himself to some chocolates.

                    ALISON

A friend of mine has a duplex on an island in the Gulf.
You fly to Tampa, rent a car from there. Believe me,
You're going to need a getaway spot if this takes off.
Which it will, once we get the hype going. I said I'd
call him back.

                    MARY

Who?

                    ALISON

Adrian. My boss. About coming up to see you. For a
rap. Mary?

                    MARY

(Points to CYST.) He's the boss.

                    ALISON

Really? I thought – Cyst? Do I have your permission?

                    CYST

(At the chocolates,) Sorry?

                    ALISON

I want to bring some people to talk to you. There's no
need to lay anything on. They can take us out to eat
for Christ's sake. It's all on the Beeb.

                    CYST

Chocolate?

                    ALISON

No thanks. Is it on? I need to call him back.

CYST crosses, offers MURIEL the chocolates.

MURIEL

Thank you, dear. May I have the cluster?

ALISON

Mary, this is serious!

MARTIN

Alison ...

ALISON

Shut up.

MARTIN

Alison!

JACK

I got one, I got one, I got one!

CYST

Jack! You angler! *(Giggles.)*

JACK

It's a big 'un! Look at the size of it!

MARY

Great!

ALISON

Look, I'm trying to set something up for you.

MURIEL

Let me see, dear.

JACK

Biggest one yet, I tell you that.

MURIEL

Oh, poor thing. Put it out of its misery.

JACK

Oh 'eck. *(Throws it back.)*

MARY

River fish, Jack. They're never good eating.

JACK

I think it's the one I caught last week.

MURIEL

Swish, swish . . . go on, wriggle.

ALISON

Please. Look will somebody talk some sense? I need to know. Forgive me for spoiling Sunday brunch, but this is important.

MARTIN

Mary, d'you mind?

MARY

Okay. As a favour to you, kid. Alison.

ALISON

Yes Mary? *(She smiles, in anticipation.)*

MARY

The answer's no.

ALISON

No? Why?

MARY

Take too long.

ALISON

But . . . look, I'm doing you a favour.

MARY

Our thanks.

ALISON

Tell me what the problem is. I'm sure we can fix it.

Francis said in the car coming up ...

MARY

I should forget that conversation.

ALISON

That's all very well. Francis was speaking for himself.
He'd like to travel. With money ... facilities ... his
life could expand. Do you think it's fair to deny him
that? We want to feature you! Look, if you're worried
about the personal appearance side, don't be. We get
scriptwriters in. It's all done on auto-cue. You read it
off a screen.

Silence.

ALISON

Francis, I'm offering you the world. Have you the
courage, the imagination to take it? You're very, very
talented. You owe something to that.

CYST looks to MARY.

MARY

Well? Answer the lady.

CYST shrugs helplessly.

MARY

What's the matter, cat got your tongue?

CYST

I don't know! What do you want me to say?

MARY

Say what you like.

ALISON

I think we should hear Cyst's point of view. I happen
to know what he feels.

MARY

Well?

CYST

They were very nice to me. They took me to tea in
Fortnums.

MARY

Bully for you.

CYST

And the opera. Fledermaus.

MARY

You were always anybody's.

CYST

You say yourself, Mary, that I'm holding you back.

MARY turns, walks away.

CYST

Whatever you want.

MARY turns, looks across at him. Slight pause.

MARY

And what do <u>you</u> want?

A long pause. They regard each other.

CYST

You know what I want.

MARY

(*Looks at him soberly, then crosses to ALISON, puts
his hands on her shoulders.*) Alison ...

ALISON

Yes?

MARY

Alison. Why don't you go and make a baby with old
Marty here?

ALISON

What? *(Decides to laugh.)* You are a big tease.

MARTIN

Leave it, Mary. *(To ALISON.)* The answer's no,
Alison. Stop being thick.

ALISON

Cyst?

CYST

Muriel?

MURIEL ponders.

MURIEL

'The violet in the mountain has split the rock.'

MARY

Tennessee Williams. One to me.

CYST

She's still winning.

ALISON

Excuse me. I mean – is that it?

MURIEL smiles up at her politely.

MARY

Seems like it, babes.

ALISON

Is that your final decision? Have you discussed it
fully? You're beyond me. Why ponce about here when
you could come in? (*Pause.*) Look, I'm offering you
the world. Talent means nothing these days. It's
presentation. I can get that for you. People would
piss blood. Well. If that's the situation. I'll leave my
number, in case you ... though I must tell you that the
offer may not last. Martin, I'd like to leave.

MARTIN

I'll see you off.

ALISON

Are you staying?

MARTIN

I want to talk to Mary.

ALISON

What about?

She grabs a book, writes her telephone number on the flyleaf,
making CYST hiss.

ALISON

(*Looks at the cover of the book.*) Oh, Proust. There's
a marvellous new translation, Mary ... I'll drop it in
next time I'm passing. (*She smiles and goes with
MARTIN.*)

JACK fishes. CYST takes another chocolate. MURIEL delves into
her embroidery bag for another skein of silk.

MURIEL

(*Sighs.*) I'm so sick of that egg-shell blue in my
bedroom.

MARY

Change it.

MURIEL

I did think of apricot.

CYST

(*Head in a book.*) Not with that lino.

MARY

Lino? Bugger lino. It's wall to wall for you, my girl.

MURIEL

Oh, get away.

MARY

You're a married woman now, Mu. There's a roll of
beige Wilton left over from 'She Stoops'. How about it?

MURIEL

I don't want to start getting soft, Mary.

MARY

(*Rises.*) And there speaks the puritan history of this
country of ours, wife. Which brings on a notion –
luncheon, anyone?

MARTIN

Yes!

JACK

You bet!

MARY

I can offer Surprise d'Agneau de Muriel ... haricots
verts, carottes mignonnes, et pommes natures. With
a Cotes du Rhone.

CYST

Evian for you.

MARY

(*Turns, surveying his kingdom.*) Et pourquoi pas, my
dear knight? (*Embracing the audience.*) Why not?

Fade to black.

The End.

UP IN SWEDEN

For Clare Davidson

UP IN SWEDEN was first performed on the 17th of October, 1975, at the Haymarket Theatre in Leicester, and subsequently, from the 27th of October to the 8th of November, at the King's Head Theatre, Islington, London, UK.

CAST

Bengt	ALAN BARKER
Karl	BILL BUFFERY
Hans	ANDREW HALL
Lars	DOMINIC JEPHCOTT
Nils	MICHAEL MALONEY

Directed by	CLARE DAVIDSON
Designed by	GILLIAN DANIELL
Stage Manager	DAVID DRUMMOND

Presented by Academy Productions

FOREWORD

There is a phrase, used in Xmas catalogues, about a certain type of recherché gift: "for the man who has everything."

To people in the Third World, we in the West have everything. We don't starve, we have access to heat, light, education, medicine, libraries, and we are free to travel. Even in our present state of recession and rising unemployment, we are affluent. And, of all the Western countries, Sweden perhaps stands, more than any other, for the 'best' of Western enlightenment. A country where there is almost no poverty; where men are allowed paternity leave; where it seems the rational obtains. Sweden, the home of the Nobel prize – gift of the armament king.

So, what is the proper stance for the young? To make more money? To live an ordered, harmonious life between the boardroom and the concert hall, and the beach-house? To rebel? Rebel against the best, in terms of comfort, that's on offer? In the Soviet Union, it is not so easy to pop down to St Tropez if you feel like it.

Most of all, what is there to resent if your parents are reasonable and enlightened liberals? After all, who needs heroes? Is a caring rationalism to be the model to follow, rather than a romantic terror? What is there to be depressed about?

Pam Gems.
June 1975

UP IN SWEDEN

ACT ONE

<u>ACT ONE – SCENE ONE</u>

LARS's Room.

The room is untidy, but with good furniture, chosen by the parents.

BENGT is lying on his back. KARL sits cross-legged. NILS hunches on the edge of the bed. LARS oils a pair of skis, and HANS stands apart. They are all eighteen.

> BENGT
>
> (*In hot argument*) I didn't say that! I didn't say that!

> NILS
>
> You did!

> BENGT
>
> I didn't! What I said was ...

> KARL
>
> You did, you know.

> NILS
>
> Of course, he ...

> KARL
>
> That's what we understood you to mean. That's what I thought you meant.

His reasonable tone placates the general mood.

BENGT

Oh Christ. (*Slight pause*) All I said was . . .

NILS

We know what you said. What you said was . . .

BENGT

Will you let me finish?

NILS

You don't have to repeat it!

BENGT

I hadn't finished!

KARL

In any case . . .

BENGT

What I was going to . . .

NILS

We know what you said. Not what you meant to say.
We know what you meant to say. What you meant to
say was . . .

BENGT

Oh, thank you.

NILS

What do you mean?

BENGT

How do you know what I meant to say when you
haven't even let me get it out? If you don't let
somebody say what they mean . . .

NILS

(*Parodies him, wagging his head*) 'There's nothing
left to protest about.'

BENGT

Oh.

NILS

That's what you meant to say. That's what you thought you said.

BENGT

Piss off.

NILS

'The trouble with Sweden is there's nothing to protest about.'

BENGT

Well, it's true.

KARL

What about the planet?

BENGT

What about the planet?

KARL

I don't know. The ozone layer?

NILS

No, that's only because we're not afraid of the Bomb anymore.

BENGT

What's that got to do with it?

NILS

There has to be a cosmic menace.

BENGT

Why?

KARL

What for?

NILS

How should I know? To placate the Devil, I daresay.

This baffles KARL and BENGT completely.

KARL

Anyway, that's not the point. (*To BENGT*)
What I want to know is, what were you on about
Stalin and Nero for? And Hitler.

BENGT

I never said Hitler.

KARL

No, I said Hitler. He's one of them, isn't he? A what-d-
you-call-it. A despot. A tyrant.

BENGT

I was trying to ...

KARL

I don't want to be like Hitler.

NILS

Why not?

KARL

You joking? (*He strokes his face lovingly.*) I'd rather
grow a full beard. (*To BENGT*) I think you're screwed
up in the role-model area, Bengt, old potato.

BENGT

I was only ... Look, people like that ... All I'm saying
is there's a logic there. They think to themselves: why
not? I might as well.

ACT ONE

KARL

Might as well? Might as well what?

BENGT

You know.

KARL

(*Honestly*) No, I don't.

NILS

What he is trying to say ... what I think he is trying
to convey, in his own inimitable,
Caliban fashion, was the Macbethian exposition.

BENGT

Eh?

NILS

Posit the meaninglessness of the world – dadada
– with existential overtones ...

BENGT

What?!

NILS

... thus predicating – via the absence of nemesis – the
maximum freedom of choice. Am I right?

BENGT

We-ell, not exactly ...

NILS

Don't bother to answer. This sally into the absurd
is highly untypical – if not downright surreal.
Especially on a Saturday afternoon.

LARS

(*Absorbed in oiling his skis*) Shuddup.

NILS

Now that is more in character.

KARL

He was only ...

LARS

Shuddup.

BENGT

If you'd only let me finish in the first place ...

LARS glares at him. He shrugs and subsides.

Pause.

KARL

My mother's still on about medical school.

NILS

Be very useful. You could help her with the genital
warts.

KARL throws a cushion at him, then lies back on the bed, with his
hands behind his head.

KARL

All right for you. She's been on the moan since my
father died. Boil on her bum last week – she went out
and made her will. I think I'll go trans- sexual. Yeah.
It's either that or the Eurovision
Song Contest. 'Nul points.' Famous for life!

BENGT looks across to LARS.

BENGT

Anyway, what are you going to do?

LARS gives him a cold look and doesn't answer.

BENGT

Hans?

LARS

(*Violent*) Shuddup!

KARL

(*To NILS*) I envy you. Heidelberg, then Berkeley.
Mind you, Paris was a disappointment.

NILS

So you said.

BENGT

Oh, why?

KARL

Got my money pinched the first day. And the
Algerians in the café all beat me at pinball.

BENGT

I think I'll go to Ecuador – or wherever the bird shit
comes from. Make a fortune.

NILS

(*To LARS*) What are you going to do?

LARS shrugs and looks across to HANS, who turns away.

LARS

How the fuck should I know? Get the fuck out of here,
I know that much.

BENGT

Join the mercenaries. Why not? My father met a man
who was in the Foreign Legion. He was telling us last
night at dinner. It was when he was in Marseilles,
putting the boat up for the winter. He went in this bar.
Actually, it was a gay bar. Being my old man, he's the

last to notice. Anyway, this guy comes up to him ...
he spoke Swedish so, naturally, they got talking. My
father said he was fantastic to look at. The whites of
his eyes, you know. He said he was really fit. Really
tough. Apparently, this guy was German. He'd been
an officer in the German army. But, in the end, he
bought himself out. He couldn't stand the strain. He
was bored shitless. Now he's a corporal in the Foreign
Legion.

                    KARL

A corporal?

                    BENGT

He told my Dad that was a respected rank. He said
it was so tough, some of them commit suicide. Two
of his lot killed themselves the first year. There's no
confinement to barracks.
All the punishments are physical.

                    LARS

They get beaten up, you mean?

                    BENGT

Yeah. Just punched out. Teeth. Jaws.
Fractured skulls.

                    KARL

Wow.

                    BENGT

They get all different nationalities. Mostly guys in
some sort of trouble. If they stick it five years, they
get a French passport. No questions asked.

                    NILS

What was he doing in the gay bar? Was he on run?

BENGT

No. He loved it! He was made a corporal after two
years. Apparently, that's almost unheard of. Almost
unknown. He said he didn't want anything else. He
was with men. He knew where he was. What he was.
And why. They'd been in Ethiopia, killing people.

HANS looks across at him briefly. Short pause.

NILS

No good for you.

BENGT

Why not?

NILS

You wouldn't last six weeks. No discos.

BENGT

He said one funny thing. He said there were two sorts
of guys. The bright ones who'd gone wrong, or made
a mess of their lives, and the thugs. It was the thugs
who cracked up, he said. I thought my father had
got it wrong, but he said no. He'd asked him again.
The really heavy guys couldn't take it. They went
bonkers. Still, I don't think I'll join.

Pause.

There is tension as HANS remains apart. Ominously still.

NILS

(*To KARL*) Didn't you go to any brothels when you
were in Paris?

KARL

(*Aside*) I told you.

BENGT

You didn't tell me. (*Sings*) 'The night they invented champagne ... It's plain as it can be ... They thought of you and me ... ' Urgh. Urgh! What was it like? Good, eh?

KARL

(*Shakes his head.*) No. They were all ugly. Either that, or a bit old, or both. Anyway, I was frightened of catching something.

BENGT

They weren't good-looking?

KARL

I went with the Algerians. They only get the ugly ones.

A pause. They brood on the future.

BENGT

(*Squeaky voice, imitating his mother.*) 'Well, why not architecture? He does lovely cartoons. Show them the one you did of grandfather.' (*Boldly, to HANS*) What are you going to do?

HANS draws his finger across his throat with a guttural sound.

LARS and NILS glance at each other.

KARL

Perhaps we should leave? Do good works in the ... I don't know ... in the jungle.

BENGT

It's not our fault! I didn't ask to be born here. Anyway, it's cold in the winter. You're not responsible for where you're born.

NILS

You're responsible for who you are.

KARL

Only partly. A lot of it's laid down. Genetics.

LARS

(*Jeering at BENGT*) True, true.

BENGT

Get off.

NILS

Not at all. Okay, the collision of the molecule in the atom is random. The second law of thermo-dynamics states inevitable chaos.

BENGT

Eh?

NILS

That things, left to themselves, collapse. Decay. But do we live by thermo-dynamics? We do not.

KARL

No?

BENGT

We live by the gun. We die by the gun. (*Makes the noise of a machine gun, followed by bomb sounds.*)

NILS

We live by the beautifully structured laws of nature. By photo-synthesis. Let there be light. (*He lies back.*) Heredity, yes. And random encounter. The step under the bus. The inhaling of a malevolent virus. But ... (*He sits up accusingly.*) ... that does not absolve us from decision. We are the problem solvers. I think it's what we're for. Don't take that religiously.

The others exchange patient glances. Nils is off again.

LARS

(*Abrupt*) So what are we going to do?

KARL

If everybody went off to do good works, it would be ridiculous. I mean, what I want to know is, when you see on television all those people like skeletons. And, you know, the doctors and nurses –the international reps who are arranging the food drops – they ain't thin, are they? So, what are they eating? And where's it coming from? I ask myself.

BENGT

They ... I suppose they have to keep themselves going. Otherwise there wouldn't be any point.

KARL

Makes you think though.

BENGT

I expect they nip off to the loo for a quick bite of choccy bar.

KARL

Anyway, what's the point of us going abroad? We haven't got any skills ... like hydroponics. We're not trained. (*To BENGT*) Are you trained?

BENGT

Don't think I feel like training. How about you, Lars?

LARS

(*Still working on his skis*) I'm training Ilse at the
moment.

BENGT

Maybe we should join some subversive movement?
Keep the revolution alive.

NILS

Ye-es. Down with commerce.

BENGT

(*Puzzled*) What?

NILS shrugs.

BENGT

My father says it's going to be us against Islam next.
He says that's where the next battle lines will be
drawn. The New Crusades. All for Sweden and the
Holy Cross!

At this, LARS mutters irritably to himself.

KARL

What did you mean – down with commerce?

NILS

What I said.

KARL

Old Lindstrom said we should be pleased everything's
going capitalistic. He said the communist centralist
dream resulted in oppression and paralysis of the
national will.

BENGT

Yeah, well, he would.

NILS

To own and to shop. To shop and to own.
Everything to be bought and sold. All life a
transaction.

KARL

I know. He said there was a danger of banality. But
that this was a problem we have to solve. That trade
was better than the old way where, when you were
short of wheat, you went in and took it off the people
in the next valley. I don't think I could kill anybody.
(*To NILS*) Could you?

NILS

I'd kill to save my own life. The lives of anybody
I cared about.

KARL

Would you? That's a surprise.

NILS

Why? We're killers. All of us.

BENGT

I'm not. And neither are you.

NILS

Yes I am.

KARL

Rubbish.

BENGT

Yeah, stop pissing about.

HANS

He means it.

Silence.

BENGT

(*To HANS*) What about you?

But HANS turns away.

NILS

We all know where he stands.

HANS

What's that supposed to mean?

NILS

You're a killer. You can't wait to do things in.

BENGT

(*Slight pause.*) Oh, come on.

KARL

(*Seeking to reduce the tension*) The warrior class,
you mean?

NILS

It's true.

HANS

Makes me perfect for the job then.

NILS

Oh, I didn't say that.

KARL

You're not supposed to enjoy it. Anyway, he's no good.
You're no good. You're too tall.

HANS

(*Irritable.*) What?

KARL

You have to be short to be a guerilla.

BENGT

Otherwise you get your arse shot off.

KARL

He could learn to crouch lower.

BENGT

No, definitely a disadvantage. Have to be you in the front line, old Karl.

KARL

I'm not killing anybody.

LARS

(*Sneers*) Not even in the cause?

KARL

Cause of what? Oh, bugger off. I couldn't even do myself in.

BENGT

Oh, that's different. I couldn't do that. It's funny but I really couldn't. Wouldn't have the nerve.
Would you?

NILS

What?

BENGT

Commit suicide.

NILS

What for?

BENGT

I didn't say what for. I said: could you do it? To yourself. Kill yourself.

NILS

Suicide's an illness. Depression.

HANS

Oh Christ! (*He turns on NILS, glaring down at him,
pale and frightening.*) Got a name for it, have you?
Got your label?

LARS

Ah, forget it.

NILS

I only said . . .

LARS

Forget it . . . professor.

BENGT

What's the matter? All he said was . . .

LARS

We heard.

HANS

Got it all sorted out? Docketed? What's the diagnosis,
Herr Doktor? What's the prognosis?
Got your prescription? Come on, what's the verdict?

NILS

Leave it.

BENGT

(*Mystified.*) I just said I couldn't do it, that's all.
That I wouldn't have the bottle.

NILS

(*Quickly*) Neither would I.

HANS

I would.

NILS

Yes, I know you would.

HANS

Oh, he knows, he knows! (*He turns away restlessly, then back to NILS.*) Well?

NILS

Well, what?

HANS

What is your response to that piece of information – that you know?

KARL

(*Nervous*) Presumably, some people have the nerve … the courage for that sort of thing. And some haven't.

HANS

Well?

NILS

Well, if you … If you, ah … If you really want to know, I find it somewhat unbearable.

HANS

Some what? Somewhat? Oh! He worries! (*He strokes NILS' face, then turns to KARL with a glittering smile.*) Do you think he's in love with me?

KARL

How should I know?

LARS

Cut it out.

NILS

In answer to that question. Yes, I think I probably am.

Silence.

HANS

Ohh! He's in love.

NILS

I don't want to kiss you. Climb into bed with you.
Screw with you.

HANS

(*Mock disappointment.*) Oh!

NILS

I'm just in love with the idea of you.

BENGT

Fucking hell.

LARS

Are you trying to be funny or something?

HANS

To think! And I never guessed. Shall we get engaged?

NILS

Piss off. I mean it. I know you're never supposed to
talk – I mean, directly. We're never, ever supposed
to say what we mean … about feelings. Dead uncool,
man. (*Heavy voice*) I mean, we are men. I don't care.
I'm changing things. Anyway, I'm too tired to keep
watching myself. We're all bloody in love with you!
Everybody you come across is yours. (*Indicates
LARS*) Yours and his. I think you'd drop dead with
shock if ever the day came … (*He pauses, and starts
again*) It's all your way. It always has been. You take

it for granted, the pair of you. You never even have to think about it! Our leaders. From the first day you came to kindergarten. Better at everything. Quicker. Stronger. Fitter. Every damn thing – easy. No bother at all. Ever. Only once. Only once did I see you sweat.

HANS

Oh?

NILS

You missed a fortnight's school when you broke your ankle.

HANS

So?

NILS

While you were away we'd begun to do calculus. You hadn't been instructed and you were baffled. I saw the sweat on your face – you were hysterical! You'd never had to try, like the rest of us, ever. Not once in your life! You didn't know how. You'd always walked it! Broke you up. Till the next lesson. You were five pages ahead of the rest of us. You'd flicked on – no trouble at all. I don't think I've ever seen you with a bloody spot on your face. Not one. (*He scratches at his own spots moodily.*)

KARL

I read somewhere that if you wash your hair with medicated shampoo ... It said spots come from dandruff falling on your face.

NILS

Bollocks, the more you wash it, the greasier it gets.

KARL

Not if you use the medicated ...

LARS

Oh, for Christ's sake!

Slight pause.

HANS

(*Savagely, to NILS*) Since you know so much, just tell
me the bloody point, that's all.

NILS

I can't.

BENGT

The point of what?

HANS

Of anything, you thick fool. I can see the point of
being a woman. Open your legs and a bloody great wet
football comes out. Follow that.

LARS

No thanks.

NILS

Maybe there is no point? Or it could be that we were
just born too late.

HANS

As I say. No point. No – point.

NILS

And doesn't that put you into a rage?

HANS

Oh?

NILS

Your fury knows no bounds.

But HANS turns away.

NILS

You're in a rage the whole time these days. A killing
rage.

BENGT

Come on . . .

LARS

Yes, why don't you leave it?

KARL

Right.

HANS

(*To KARL*) Are you a monster?

Slight pause.

KARL

I don't think so. No.

NILS

Of course we are.

The others look baffled.

NILS

Haven't you noticed the way they treat us?

KARL

Who?

NILS

(*Snarls*) Them! Under all the mateyness and the
advice. Oh God, the advice. They're not like that with
the girls. Girls are easy. All you have to do is raise

your voice. Besides, they're nice to have around.
Decorative. (*Winning tones*) 'Hull-o! What can we do
for you?'

KARL

BENGT

To you. Hahaha!

KARL

I don't know what you mean.

NILS

Yes, you do. The way they try to keep us in hand. The
way they want us to join. What is it to be old chap,
university, the army? It's not too early to talk about
pension schemes. Planning – that's the thing! Pin us
down. In case we ... break out or something. (*He looks
up at HANS*) It's like we've got guns to their heads.
God knows what's wrong with my father. Every time I
come into the room, he gets up and leaves.

The other laugh loudly.

KARL

I've told you. Change your shampoo.

BENGT

I know what he means. My old man – fat-arsed little
prick – I could knock him down when I was twelve.
What does he bother for?

KARL

Your uncle Bertil's even shorter. He's done all right
for himself. Three wives and a house in Lanzarote.
No flies on him.

BENGT

Yeah, he'll have to go. He wears mirror sunglasses. I
fancy getting one of those rifles that comes in a black

attaché case, and you slot it all together. Click, click, click. Boom, boom.

LARS

(*Lazily*) You'd wash your face in poop if somebody told you to.

BENGT

What do you mean?

LARS and BENGT wrestle in an unfriendly fashion. When the scuffle begins to get nasty, HANS gives BENGT a kick that lifts him across the room.

He and LARS glare at each other.

Then BENGT takes out a comb and combs his hair.

NILS

No. Trouble is, we've messed up Darwinism. In the old days, all the weaklings pegged out. They didn't make it. I mean, two hundred years ago, you two ... (*He waves a hand at LARS and HANS*) Well, there were plenty of wars. Work for guys like you. Swords. Horses. Death or glory. Now, everything's technical. A bloody girl can press a button.

BENGT

Nah, nah, nah. Plenty about still.

NILS

What?

BENGT

Formula One.

KARL

The Olympics. (*Hates to contradict Nils*) Sorry.

BENGT

There's that twit who keeps going to the North
Pole, and his toes fall off. Eeny, meeny, miney mo ...

HANS

(*Under his breath*) Fuck, fuck, fuck, fuck, fuck, fuck,
fuck, fuck, fuck ...

NILS

Rubbish, of course. All the causes aren't over.
There's everything to conquer ... discover ...

HANS

Fuck, fuck ...

NILS

More people are killed by natural disasters ...

NILS slows to a stop as HANS continues to mutter to himself.

They all look at him covertly. He seems to have forgotten their
presence. He bangs his hand against the wall.

KARL

I know what you mean. But what if you don't want ...
I mean, I don't want to save anybody. Cure people.
You have to want to. What I want is an exciting life.
But without any danger. I want to live. I want to live
glamorously. But how can you? Except by going into
the movies, and that's silly. I mean, it wouldn't fool
you, would it? Dressing up and farting about. Waiting
for the stuntman to come and fall off your horse. It's
okay for getting women. That's why it's so popular. My
French friend, Antoine's only a second cameraman
and he does really well.

Pause.

BENGT

I think I'll push off.

NILS

(*To HANS*) What happened to Paola?

HANS doesn't reply. NILS turns to LARS.

NILS

(*To LARS*) What happened to Paola?

LARS

How should I know? Bloody girls.

BENGT

Yeah. they get above themselves. I was with Mai the other night. All she does is talk, talk, talk, and make leather earrings. She'd been down the Skagen Club with all those lesbians. What do they get up to that's so marvellous? I don't believe in it. It's just a lot of dykes showing off.

LARS

Shall we go down there? Rape the lot of them?

BENGT

Yeah!

KARL

Why not?

NILS

No. They'd only make a fuss.

Murmurs of agreement.

BENGT

Bloody women.

Pause.

                    NILS

What then?

                    BENGT

God knows.

                    KARL

Maybe it's exam fever. Maybe we shouldn't do
anything? Just mooch around for a bit. Get our
bearings. What's the rush?

                    HANS

It's got to stop.

                    LARS

What?

                    HANS

Everything.

He bangs his hand on the table, making everything shake.

                    HANS

Wake up. Get out of bed. Don't wash. Don't clean your
fucking teeth. Crap. Eat. Screw.Ride the fucking bike.
Read a fucking magazine. It has to stop.

                    NILS

How?

                    HANS

By not going on with it.

Pause.

                    BENGT

What do you think we should do Nils?

NILS

(*Mimicking him with sudden irritability.*) 'Whatshall
we do, Nils?' Make up your own bloody mind!

He rolls over on the divan, facing the wall.

LARS

Go round the world on a raft . . . backwards?

KARL

Sideways . . .

BENGT

Nils?

KARL

Yeah, come on, you must have some idea. All right for
you – sodding off to university.

BENGT

Bet he ends up a teacher.

NILS

That's right. I've sold out. Thank you one and all. Why
don't you ask him? (*Pointing an accusing finger*) He's
your leader – fucking
Hercules over there.

BENGT

Genghis Khan, you mean?

KARL

Ivan the Terrible?

NILS

Attila the fucking Hun. Ask him!

KARL

Okay. If you say so. What shall we do, Hans?

LARS

Good question. I'm buggered if I know.

NILS

Tell them, Hans.

BENGT

Yeah, we always do what you want. Tell us.

HANS turns to face them. He looks at them each in turn.

HANS

You want me to tell you?

CHORUS

Yes!

HANS

You want me to tell you what to do?

CHORUS

Yes!!

HANS

(*To NILS*) You?

NILS

(*After a slight pause*) All right.

HANS

Everybody swears, right?

CHORUS

Yes.

Pause.

BENGT

Okay?

KARL

The suspense is killing me.

LARS

What are we going to do?

HANS moves away. He turns, looks at LARS, then across to NILS.

NILS

What's the matter?

HANS

I was wondering if you could bear to take that glistening look off your face.

NILS

What?

HANS

You heard me.

NILS

I honestly don't know what you mean.

HANS

'Honestly?'

NILS

No, I don't! What do you mean?

HANS

Nothing.

NILS

No, come on. You can't. (*He shrugs*) Just tell us.

HANS

You know already.

NILS

Know? Of course I don't know! How should I know?

HANS

Don't you?

NILS

What are you talking about? I'm not a bloody mind reader.

HANS

Oh, I thought you were.

Pause.

BENGT

Come on!

HANS

(*Indicating NILS*) He'll tell you.

KARL

What?

BENGT

I thought you were going to.

LARS

We don't want his . . .

HANS

I'm right, aren't I?

HANS stands over NILS with a cold smile. NILS looks up at him, then rolls off the divan and moves away.

HANS

Well?

NILS

Perhaps. Perhaps not.

HANS

You fucking know. You always fucking know.

You know it all, don't you? You make it your business,
you crap, shit-eater. I hope it gives you pleasure.
Satisfaction.

NILS

I'm not always right. I'm often wrong.

HANS

Not this time. Tell them.

A chorus of disappointment.

NILS

Why me?

HANS

I just want to know if you're right.

NILS

(*Quick*) He wants to kill us.

KARL

What?

LARS

What are you talking about?

BENGT

Yeah, what is this? Some sort of joke?

NILS

Sit down, Bengt. You make me tired when you stand
up. He wants to kill us. (*He looks at HANS*) Right?

HANS bows ironically, then sits abruptly, as if suddenly exhausted.

BENGT

Bloody hell. (*He bursts out laughing.*)

KARL

Shut up. (*To NILS*) I'm sorry. I don't understand.
What do you mean?

NILS

I thought I made myself pretty clear.

KARL

But, why? I mean, how? I mean, what are you talking
about? All of us?

HANS

Not necessarily. (*Tired*) One of you, if you like.

KARL

I see.

BENGT

Draw lots, you mean?

LARS

(*Violently*) No!

KARL

(*To LARS*) What do you mean? No, not draw lots, or
no, it's a bad idea, or … ?

LARS jerks KARL's head back cruelly, and let's go. KARL howls
with pain.

LARS

Shut up! (*To HANS*) Who?

KARL

(*Rubbing his neck*) Oww!

HANS

Who do you think? (*Loses energy*) I don't really care.
It's all the same to me.

LARS

Well, so long as you don't expect me to ...

BENGT

You can count me out!

LARS

If I really thought you ...

NILS

He's not asking you.

LARS

Oh?

NILS

No.

LARS glares at him, coldly.

NILS

He's asking me.

Silence.

BENGT

Oh, come on.

NILS

That's right, isn't it?

HANS doesn't reply.

NILS

That's what you want.

HANS

Not at all. It's what you want.

NILS

(*Shocked*) No! I don't want that. No way!

HANS

I see. Then, suppose I were to ask you, in any case?

NILS

The answer would be no.

HANS

Suppose that the circumstances . . .

NILS

Under no circumstances.

HANS

If I were dying. Of TB . . . or cancer . . .

NILS

It doesn't apply. You're not.

HANS

As always, the flight to the concrete.

NILS

There isn't an exam – a test you couldn't have
beaten me in. If you could have been bothered, you
contemptuous bastard. Why should I do anything for
you?

HANS

You're the one.

Silence.

NILS

Well, I'm sorry. The answer's no.

HANS

(*Softly*) Can't I persuade you?

NILS

Absolutely not.

HANS

You won't reconsider?

NILS shakes his head.

NILS

No.

HANS

(*A terrifying screaming roar*) Well, somebody then!!!

The others are shocked into appalled silence. Their mouths drop open and they draw away from HANS, shocked.

HANS

Kill me! (*He wheels, roaring.*) Kill me!!!

He stands, centre-stage, mad.

A long pause. He stands there, head lowered, grinding his teeth, eyes rolling.

KARL

(*Whispers*) What is it? Is he trying to be funny? I'm sorry, I just don't think this is a joke.

HANS looks at KARL, and speaks in a quiet, normal voice.

HANS

He thinks I'm joking. (*He crosses to NILS, and pushes him slightly.*) Tell him.

But NILS shakes his head. He is unable to speak. He gives HANS a swift look, and turns away.

BENGT

Look ... (*He clears his throat.*) Look, we've always done things together. Ever since kindergarten. (*Clears his throat again.*) What's going on?

KARL

No, I'm sorry. We're not in this together. If it's not just fooling around. Anyway, nobody in their right mind ... If he really feels ... if he's that miserable, he should see a doctor. I'm sorry, I don't know what's going on.

LARS

(*To HANS*) Why him?

HANS

(*Shrugs*) I just want him to kill me, that's all. If not him, all right, you ... all of you. I don't care. Suit yourselves. (*Slight pause*) We're supposed to be friends.

Pause.

BENGT

It's all very well, mate. But we'd get into trouble for it.

HANS

Not if you got rid of the body.

NILS

How are we supposed to do that?

HANS

It's only meat, for God's sake. Offal. Bury it in the forest. (*He flicks a quick look at NILS' blanched face.*)

NILS stares back at im steadily.

NILS

Animals would dig you up.

HANS

Chuck it in the incinerator.

BENGT

Oh, very clever! What the hell do you weigh? What
are we supposed to do? Take you along to the
butcher's? Oh, how much do you charge to joint
people? Very funny.

LARS

Lay off.

BENGT

Anyway, it's a daft idea ... you'd smell. I remember
poor old Gunnar. You could smell roast dinner before
they got the car off the track. I was right behind
him ...

ALL

Yeah, yeah. All right, Bengt.

They've obviously heard him recount this story many times.

BENGT

It was not being able to get him out. The bloody doors
were glowing – white hot!

KARL

It wasn't your fault.

LARS

We could throw you in the lake, with weights.
(*He's decided this is a game, and he's going to play.*)
No, that wouldn't do. You might get fished up. It's not
deep enough. (*He grins, wolfish.*) We could eat you.

BENGT

Get off.

HANS

Ye-es. Yes, that might work. (*To NILS*) What do you
think?

NILS

I think nothing. It's not worth talking about.

HANS

Oh, why not? It's rather a good idea.

NILS

No.

HANS

Why not?

NILS

What's in it for me?

HANS

Take your pick. Fillet, porterhouse, chump . . .

NILS

I'm a vegetarian.

KARL

So am I. Well, except for eggs and fish. And
sometimes . . .

NILS

(*Ignoring him*) I am also agnostic. I do not, therefore,
believe that if I ate your thigh, mine would be more
beautiful or efficient. Nor that, if I ate your eye,
mine too would be cobalt blue. Even if I believed it, it
wouldn't happen. It's Lamarckian . . . ergo, nothing
in it for me. Dead, you are of no interest. Alive, you
keep me going, one way or another. Even if it's just
to mop up your cast-offs. Even when I know you

can beat me at anything you care to mention. Even
that, because … because … I have a notion that,
despite your bloody looks, and your style, and your
remorseless intelligence, and your fucking, fucking
facility, I may … I may, in the end, just tread right
over you. Because, in the end, mine is the better
position. Because, in the end, I want it. There's a cause
in it. A runner ahead. An obstacle. An impossibility.
I shall beat you, just as I have always beaten you.
Just as I always will. Me and my sort. You're there
for me to knock down. I need you. Why should I
involve myself in Gotterdammerung? I don't need the
twilight of the Gods. There's nothing in it for me.

HANS

You were always a bloody dealer.

NILS

Yes.

HANS

I need someone.

NILS

(*Nods towards LARS*) Let him do it. He's the buddy.
The acolyte.

HANS

I'd rather it was you.

NILS

(*Loses it*) For God's sake, why?!

HANS

You're more methodical. You play by the rules. (*Slight
pause.*) It would need your help.

NILS

I'm flattered.

HANS

You're efficient.

NILS

Lars is efficient.

BENGT

(*Jeers*) Lars?

NILS

He gets what he wants. A dapper man, Lars.

HANS

Hah! Just the same, not Lars.

KARL

Because you're friends, you mean?

BENGT

Oh, come on! This has gone far enough.

KARL

It's because they're friends. They're still ganging
up on us. I don't see why we should protect Lars – do
Lars's dirty work. Anyway, with you (*He points at
HANS*) … out of the way, he'll be top man. I'd rather
have you. Lars has a mean streak.

LARS kicks out at him sideways.

KARL

See what I mean? (*He picks himself up.*)
That's how it would be, wouldn't it?

NILS

Lars ascendant.

HANS

Not necessarily.

BENGT

Oh, come on!

HANS

Not Lars.

NILS

You surprise me. The spirit if Beau Geste is no more.
Eheu fugaces. Alas, the fleeting years slip by.

HANS

Don't be more of a prick than you are.

BENGT

Well, if Nils won't do it, I'm not doing it. (*Slight pause.*)
Or, you could do it yourself. Why not? Do yourself in.
Then we're not involved. There's drugs. Distalgesic.
Or you could jump off the building. Of course,
you might not kill yourself. You might end up a
quadriplegic. You could go in for the cripple Olympics.
You'd do well. Let me think. I know, you could run
your CBX 1000 into a brick wall. No, same again. You
might just end up a drooling idiot. (*He imitates brain
damage.*) Yuh! Yuh!

KARL

Shut up! (*To HANS*) Why don't you go off and join
something? Be a bloody guerilla in South America, I
don't know. At least you've got a chance!

HANS

Chance?

KARL

Oh, it's useless. He's useless when he's like this.

I think it's totally self-indulgent the way you let
yourself get depressed and drag everybody else
down with you. It's not fair. You've got everything!
You can do anything you want! I also happen to
know that you're kind. All right, I'm not going to
tell. That's half your trouble,Hans. You're so afraid
of being seen to be human. You seem to think it's
some kind of weakness. There are different sorts of
courage, you know. Anyway, it's imperialist, refusing
to accept help. If you want to know, it gets up my
nose. (*Slight pause.*) All right! It's all very well being
anti-everything. It's easy! What's hard is ... I mean,
now we're going to have to get down to it. Throw our
caps in the ring. What are we for? I mean, I'm fucked
if I know. But there's a hell of a lot out there. Just
look around. As a species, we're just crawling out of
the slime. I just wish somebody would tell me what's
going on here. Nobody ever tells me.

                    NILS
There's no conspiracy.

                    KARL
Isn't there?

                    HANS
Are you going to do it or not?

                    NILS
I can't.

                    HANS
Why?

                    NILS
I don't want to.

HANS

I thought you were a friend.

NILS

I owe you a lot of favours. I'm aware of that.

HANS

Not the same thing.

NILS

Oh, all right. Yes, we're friends. And enemies.

HANS

(*A wintry smile*) That should make it easier.

NILS

You permit me to enjoy myself. (*Angry*) Thank you!

HANS

I'm sorry. I didn't mean that.

NILS

You're full of shit.

HANS

Just do it.

NILS

Please don't ask.

HANS

I can't go on.

NILS

I know that.

BENGT

What you need is a new woman, Hans.

NILS

Give it time.

HANS

Time? Time! There isn't any. There is no more time!

HANS sits, his head against the wall, eyes closed.

LARS, offended at having been rejected for Nils, speaks coldly.

LARS

You have been getting wild lately.

HANS

(*To NILS*) Please ...

NILS

Why me, for God's sake? Why should I ruin myself?
It's too much! Stick a shotgun in your mouth. Go
and jump off the Blue Mountain. Sit in the car with a
hosepipe on the exhaust. Why do you want me to do
it? Why does it have to be me?

BENGT

Because you're the brains, Nils. We always come to
you.

NILS

The bloody caretaker, you mean. My life's bloody
staked out for me before I begin!

HANS

An act of friendship. That's all I ask. I need help.

KARL

No. It's gone far enough. Either get off it, or
I'm leaving.

No-one responds. KARL picks up his coat but no-one moves.

KARL exits.

BENGT

Sodding little twit. He'll be back.

LARS

Bugger off.

BENGT exits.

NILS

Now what? You can't force me.

HANS

Just do it.

NILS

Why?

HANS

(*Mutters*) Do it.

NILS

Why?! (*Then softly*) Why? I have to know why.
Can't you see that? Tell me why.

HANS

(*Surprised*) I thought you knew.

NILS

Perhaps, but I'm not sure. I need to know if I know.

HANS

Is that a bargain?

NILS

Tell me why.

HANS

Because ... because if you don't. If you say no ... If
you won't do it, I shall go home. Go into my father's
study. Get his shotgun and the rifle. And I shall

go down into the street and mow down as many
children as I see.

NILS

(*After a pause.*) All right. In that case ... in that case,
I'll do whatever you want.

HANS unsheathes a KNIFE and hands it to him.

HANS

If you push here, like this, upwards – and give it a
twist. That should do it.

LARS

You'll make a mess.

HANS

Not if he does it right. The blood will stop flowing as
soon as he gets to the heart. Find a towel, if you're
worried.

LARS

Right.

LARS exits.

HANS and NILS are left alone, both on their feet, confronting each
other. HANS is smiling slightly.

Enter LARS with a ridiculously domestic-looking towel in bright
pink and yellow, with flowers.

LARS

Is this all right?

HANS

(*Without looking*) Oh Christ.

HANS and NILS exchange a brief, exclusive smile.

LARS spreads the towel at their feet.

LARS

(*His voice thick*) All right?

They look down briefly and nod.

NILS

Yes, that's fine. (*To HANS*) Are you ready?

HANS

Yes, I'm ready.

NILS

No farewell speech?

HANS

(*Voice thickened.*) You always were, and you always will be, a second-rate, time-serving, pedantic little shit.

NILS

I'm sorry. I apologise. I don't know what made me say that. It was totally out of place. Put it down to nerves.

HANS

Get on with it.

NILS

I've always known you despised me. But then you despise all of us, don't you?

He holds the knife at HANS. He makes him wait for it.

He makes him wait a long time.

At last, at the very moment when it looks as though HANS might crack, NILS slashes him down one cheek.

HANS howls loudly, bellowing like an animal, and claps his hand to his face. He whimpers with pain.

NILS

(*Crisp*) There. That should do it.

HANS staggers, blinded by his own blood.

LARS

Christ!

NILS

Come on. Come on, come on ...

NILS waves the knife wildly, slicing the air.

LARS backs away in alarm.

LARS

Christ!

NILS jumps on the bed, waving the knife.

NILS

Come on down! Come and join the rest of us, the
second-class squits!

LARS

Christ, he looks terrible.

NILS

He looks marvellous!

NILS jumps down towards HANS and LARS.

LARS

Get out. Put the bloody thing down! Have you gone
mad?!

NILS

Do you want me to do the other side? Do you want
to be evened up? Come on ... While we're about it ...
Make a job of it!

HANS looks up at him through his fingers, bloodied and weeping with shock.

NILS surveys him.

> NILS
>
> What are you, in the end? You make me puke.
> (*He throws the KNIFE away.*) I've no time for it. (*He looks back at HANS and concern takes over.*) Oh God.

HANS, on his knees, weeps quietly.

> NILS
>
> Come on. Come on, love. You're all right. All over now. Stitch you up, you'll be as right as rain.

> LARS
>
> What the hell!

But HANS nods slowly, looking up at NILS.

> NILS
>
> Come on. You're losing blood. (*He helps HANS to his feet.*) We'd better get you to a hospital.

> HANS
>
> (*Mumbles*) Thanks.

> NILS
>
> Bring his coat.

> HANS
>
> I mean it.

> LARS
>
> What?!

> NILS
>
> That's all right. You'd do the same for me.

HANS

(*With a terrible smile*) Beau Geste?

In pain, HANS tries not to laugh. NILS laughs with him. LARS gapes at them.

NILS

(*To LARS*) His coat. (*To HANS*) Come on.

NILS helps HANS out.

LARS stands, bloodied and bewildered. Then he remembers the coat, and looks around. He finds HANS's coat – a beautiful, new SKIING JACKET in shining blue and green.

He gazes at it for a second, still baffled, and then throws it over his arm, and follows the others.

Fade to black.

The End.

AFTERWORD

Pam Gems was labelled a feminist writer – sometimes even a 'post-feminist' writer – but she was more than that. Feminism, for her, was only one aspect of a larger picture: the dissolution and transmogrification of Western Society.

CAMILLE, THE BLUE ANGEL and THE ODD WOMEN were nineteenth century novels she adapted, in large part, because of their value in showing us the fixed society that had come before.

Pam was born in 1925, in a semi-rural part of England that, in many respects, still resembled the Victorian age – with big houses inhabited by aristocrats and forelock-tugging servants, while the poor living in hovels on the edge of starvation, dependent on alms from the Church.

As a young teenager, she worked in a factory straight out of Dickens's *Hard Times*. At eighteen, she joined the WRENS, and witnessed the radical changes brought about by WW2, which put the Attlee government in power – a revolutionary government intent upon putting an end to the class system.

The idiocies of the 'officer class,' had taught the people they were just as capable (if not more capable) than the mentally ill upper-crusters who had commanded them during the war.

At the same time, a loss of faith in the Church (not least because of its class arrogance) created a vacuum that filled with nihilism, hedonism, muddled dreams of a socialist utopia, and a new philosophy – Existentialism – which preached that meaning and purpose weren't conferred by Church or State but by each person individually.

In short, the fixed structure of society, painstakingly established over more than a thousand years, was shattered. The only constants remaining, apart from the basic instinct to survive, were Christmas, football, and the biological imperative to reproduce.

After the war, society atomized into nuclear families, each one a small boat on a vast ocean. Only the ultra-rich, at the top of society, retained the extended family and its cohesive customs and traditions. The rest of us were on our own.

And when the contraceptive pill was deployed in the 1960's, together with cures for syphilis and the media promotion of 'free love,' the nuclear family itself came under stress.

At the end of the '60's, the British divorce rate was 6%. By the end of the '70's, it was 52%, and single-parent families, once a rarity, were commonplace.

To compound this dissolution of structure, governments tore down what they called 'slum neighborhoods' (often well-built Victorian terraced cottages with gardens) replacing them with high-rise blocks, thus destroying local communities. Public services established by church-going Victorians and Edwardians, such as public swimming baths, public laundries, common land, cricket and football pitches, parks, public benches, and public toilets were sold off to property developers and banks. The police were taken off the beat, their mission changed to serving the state rather than the people in their local communities.

And, while this was happening, non-enforcement of the monopoly laws led to the decimation of small and medium-sized businesses, the destruction of our once-thriving high streets by chain-stores and supermarkets, and the devouring of family farms by large, élite-owned, agribusiness combines.

The dismantling of British society further accelerated with the removal of its borders and sovereignty when annexed by the European Union. New taxes were imposed, such as V.A.T., to feed the EU. Thousands of new regulations were imposed. Unelected assemblies were installed to manage

Britain's EU-designated regions. Large, well-rooted communities in Wales, the Midlands, and the North were wiped out by the government complying with EU policies that demanded war on the coal-mining, ship-building, car, steel and fishing industries, resulting in the collapse of yet more indigenous communities.

To add to Britain's woes, the world's poor were encouraged to flood into the country, and the indignation this produced was nastily branded as 'racist' by state authorities and the complicit corporate media. The same corporate media that disparaged Britain's imperialist past, while it strenuously promoted the imperialism of the European Union.

The insecurity and anxiety produced by these all-out attacks on British society were treated with drugs from a ruthlessly profiteering chemical industry and, an expanding and invasive bureaucracy of apparatchiks and social workers.

Pam Gems perceived all this and offered insights, theories, and options. Although women were her primary concern, her philosophy equally embraced the challenges facing men.

In GARIBALDI, SI! she presents an idealized picture of a man in the fullness of his manhood. In UP IN SWEDEN, she portrays the terrifying void facing young men. She further delves into issues confronting men in LOVING WOMEN, FRANZ INTO APRIL, THE SOCIALISTS, and STANLEY.

Pam Gems made it her mission to write good parts for women and to support women playwrights and directors but, in the Ibsen tradition, her fundamental purpose was in diagnosing the realities, delusions, and maladies of our times.

Jonathan Gems

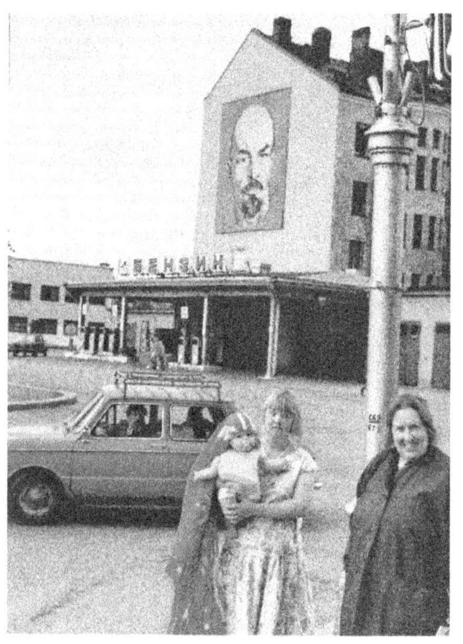

Pam Gems and her daughter, Lala,
in the Soviet Union, 1986.

Other plays in print.

CAMILLE   (Bloomsbury)
DUSA, FISH, STAS and VI   (Bloomsbury)
MARLENE   (Bloomsbury)
MRS PAT   (Bloomsbury)
PIAF   (Bloomsbury)
QUEEN CHRISTINA   (Bloomsbury)
THE LADY FROM THE SEA   (Bloomsbury)
THE LITTLE MERMAID   (Bloomsbury)
THE SNOW PALACE   (Bloomsbury)
YERMA   (Bloomsbury)
STANLEY   (Nick Hern Books)
THE SEAGULL   (Nick Hern Books)
UNCLE VANYA   (Nick Hern Books)
THE CHERRY ORCHARD   (Cambridge University Press)

Bloomsbury   www.bloomsbury.com
Nick Hern Books   www.nickhernbooks.co.uk
Cambridge University Press   www.cambridge.org

Q

website: www.quotabooks.com
email: info@quotabooks.com
Twitter: @Quotabooks